WOMEN, MEN
AND
TIME

Recent Titles in
Contributions in Women's Studies

Women, Men and Time

GENDER DIFFERENCES IN PAID WORK, HOUSEWORK AND LEISURE

Beth Anne Shelton

CONTRIBUTIONS IN WOMEN'S STUDIES,
NUMBER 127

GREENWOOD PRESS
Westport, Connecticut
London

Library of Congress Cataloging-in-Publication Data

Shelton, Beth Anne.
    Women, men and time : gender differences in paid work, housework
and leisure / Beth Anne Shelton.
        p. cm.—(Contributions in women's studies, ISSN 0147–104X ;
no. 127)
    Includes bibliographical references and index.
    ISBN 0–313–26512–7 (alk. paper)
    1. Sexual division of labor—United States. 2. Women—Employment—
United States. 3. Women—United States—Time management. 4. Men—
United States—Time management. 5. Work and family—United States.
6. Home economics—United States. I. Title. II. Series.
HD6060.65.U5S54   1992
306.3′615′0973—dc20   91–36332

British Library Cataloguing in Publication Data is available.

Library of Congress Catalog Card Number: 91–36332
ISBN: 0–313–26512–7
ISSN: 0147–104X

First published in 1992

Greenwood Press, 88 Post Road West, Westport, CT 06881
An imprint of Greenwood Publishing Group, Inc.

Printed in the United States of America

The paper used in this book complies with the
Permanent Paper Standard issued by the National
Information Standards Organization (Z39.48–1984).

10 9 8 7 6 5 4 3 2

For Ben and Sarah

Contents

Tables

Preface

When I graduated in 1984 my intent was to avoid the study of gender. I was interested in examining inequality but had determined that I could do so with relatively little reference to gender. At the time, it seemed that if I did not focus on gender I would not be hired as the "woman to teach sex roles." Although I think I have avoided being hired as the "woman to teach sex roles" my intention not to study gender only lasted one year.

After I graduated I studied economic inequality and focused on earnings. Gender was always such an important factor in determining earnings that it became obvious that I had to examine the role of gender more fully. Fine, I thought. Studying how gender impacts on earnings is acceptable and different than "really" studying gender.

Eventually it occurred to me that simply to acknowledge the association between gender and earnings was insufficient; thus I began to focus on why gender and earnings were related. When examining the relationship between gender and earnings I became interested in the argument that the association existed because women were more "committed" to the household and less "committed" to the labor market than men. This commitment could, some scholars argued, be seen in women's greater time spent in the household on housework and childcare. This led me to investigate the impact of women's household labor time on their earnings. When I began studying this relationship I was convinced that women's household labor time would have little relationship to their earnings. Women could not, I hoped, "deserve" to earn less than men. I was surprised and initially dismayed to discover that women's household labor time explained some of the earnings gap even after other characteristics had been taken into account. Clearly, what occurred in the household affected what went on in the labor market. At this time I still convinced myself that I was studying inequality, but I was beginning to understand that I was also studying gender and that I could teach the "gender classes" anyway.

As I thought about the relationship between women's household labor time and their earnings, the distribution of household labor and how it occurred began to interest me. Rather than simply assuming that women chose to spend time on housework and childcare, I became interested in the determinants of the household division on labor, initially to understand how household processes affected labor market ones, but later because the division of labor in the household was interesting in itself. As I became more interested in gender roles I also began to look for indicators of gender roles other than attitude measures. Using time-use indicators, I began to examine factors affecting the division of labor in the household, as well as how the division of labor in the household affected women's earnings and participation in the labor market. After several years of writing articles pertaining to various aspects of connection among household labor, paid labor and leisure, it seemed appropriate to write a more systematic account of the patterns of men's and women's time use.

When I began to write this book I intended to use the 1975-81 Study of Time Use (STU). As I began the research, however, I became aware of the National Survey of Families and Households (NSFH) and decided to add it to my data base. Although the NSFH contained data only on paid labor time and household labor time, it provided more recent data and measures that were similar enough to the STU measures that some comparisons could be made. At this point, I decided the project was feasible and began writing the book. I have written a book that (1) describes time use over time; (2) clarifies gender differences in time use and change in time use; (3) identifies some of the sources of the gender gap in time use and the prospects for reducing the gap.

Acknowledgments

Ben Agger encouraged me to write the book, read numerous drafts and provided much needed and appreciated moral support. My collaboration on other research with Juanita Firestone helped me formulate the plans for the book. Thanks to Steven Nock and Marjorie Starrels for offering helpful comments at various stages of the writing. My research assistant, Mary Crawford, worked on the project from the beginning. In addition to spending hours on tedious computer work, she offered valuable comments on earlier drafts. I am lucky to have completed this project before she graduated.

Thanks to Kate Hausbeck and Laurie Lanning for volunteering to type and print tables under time pressure and to Laurie Rhodebeck for lending me books and listening to me complain. I also owe thanks to a number of undergraduates who worked as my work-study students. Carol Brink, Paul Fuller, Julia Thuha Pham and Marcy Wong did library research. Ann Beutel helped with the data analysis.

Richard Kucharski of the Academic Computing Center at SUNY-Buffalo saved "destroyed" tapes and otherwise offered technical assistance far beyond what I could reasonably expect.

1

Introduction

THE PROBLEM AND THE LITERATURE

In March 1991, CBS announced that Meredith Viera would not be allowed to continue her part-time status as a correspondent on "60 Minutes." Viera joined "60 Minutes" in 1989 as a part-time correspondent to partially replace the departing Diane Sawyer. She negotiated the unprecedented part-time position, and a lower salary, because of childbearing and childrearing responsibilities. Pregnant again, she sought to extend this part-time arrangement. Her predicament, as she describes it, is that she is a woman of childbearing age (Sporkin and Speidel, 1991). For her part, Sawyer reportedly left "60 Minutes" so she could spend more time with her husband.

Sawyer's choice and Viera's problem are visible examples of the conflicting demands faced by many women in the 1990s. Job demands are not often tailored to accommodate household demands. Moreover, women are far more likely to face these dual demands than are men. Certainly, there are some very visible examples of women who have successfully negotiated job and household demands—Jane Pauley, Mary Alice Williams—but we see few men facing these challenges or seeking changes in job requirements in order to accommodate their household responsibilities, or in response to their biological clocks.

We do know that some women manage the dual demands of employment and housework through creative scheduling of their days. They may, for example, sacrifice weekend leisure time to household demands (Meissner et al., 1975). Thus, even those women who manage to coordinate paid work and household demands may lose leisure time in order to do so. Other women may be unable successfully to coordinate paid work and household or childbearing demands. Connie Chung and Meredith Viera are examples of women who have, in some sense, failed to accommodate work and family roles. Connie Chung is a visible example of a woman who postponed having children until she was in her forties and subsequently had difficulty conceiving a child. Her postponement reflects the demands of her job and the difficulty in accommodating a full-time job in the paid labor force to the demands of a household, and particularly a household with children. Meredith Viera has ultimately failed to balance her dual responsibilities as she would like; her career is suffering because of her household responsibilities and childbearing choices.

While men are visibly absent from the current discussions about work and family roles, their absence attests to their success in compartmentalizing or minimizing the demands of the household. Few men feel forced to choose between paid labor and family responsibilities, partially because the "responsibilities" of a family may be seen to be different for men than for women. Rather than contributing time to the family, men may contribute financial resources. At the same time, men rarely must choose different jobs so that they can minimize travel time and spend time with a spouse, as Diane Sawyer did when she left "60 Minutes" in 1989.

In spite of the apparent conflict among women's work, housework and leisure roles in the 1990s, and the lack of conflict among men's roles, the very fact that these issues are finding their way onto the pages of our newspapers and magazines may signify important social changes. In addition, some women's successes in balancing work and family may reflect the changed priorities of their partners. Jane Pauley's thirteen years on the "Today

Show," as well as the birth of three children, tells us something about NBC but it also tells us something about her husband. The recent changes in women's employment patterns and the subsequent pressures on the family, and on men, require us to examine just how men's and women's time use is changing.

This book addresses women's and men's roles by examining their time investments in household labor, paid labor and leisure. Time investments are studied over time, and the factors associated with different patterns of time use are examined as well. This study builds on previous research that both describes and analyzes women's and men's roles in a variety of ways.

A qualitative scholarly description of the dual demands of the labor market and the household can be found in Arlie Hochschild's *The Second Shift* (1989). Here Hochschild documents the reality of conflicting demands by examining their impact on a sample of families. Hochschild spent time with the families in her study and is able to provide detailed descriptions of how they cope, and fail to cope, with the demands of work and family. In addition, changing gender roles have been the subject of more systematic research since 1970 (e.g., Pleck, 1985). The impetus for much of this research is the change in women's and men's roles in the labor force. Significant increases in women's labor force participation rates, as well as in the rates at which women participate in the labor force full-time, challenge traditional notions of women's primary exclusion from the labor market as well as assumptions about their responsibility for the family (England and Farkas, 1986; Gershuny and Robinson, 1988). As Pleck (1985) and others have argued, the change in women's labor force participation raises questions not only about the assumptions regarding women's roles but also about men's roles in the labor market and household (Robinson, 1988).

The obvious changes in women's and men's roles in the labor market, and the assumptions about the probable consequences of these changes for the household, have encouraged sociologists to examine these changes more precisely as well as to assess their implications. Various researchers have examined changing roles in the labor market, sex role attitudes, men's reactions to the changes in women's labor market roles, the implications of changes in women's labor force participation for the division of labor in the household and, to some extent, the leisure implications of women's dual roles in the labor market and in the household.

In examining women's changing roles in the paid labor force the primary focus has been on the impact of changes in household composition and women's characteristics. For example, sociologists have examined the extent to which smaller family size can account for some of the increase in women's labor force participation (Lorence, 1987; Robinson, 1977, 1988). As the average number of children per family declined in the last half of the twentieth century, researchers sought to determine whether the presumed reduction in housework associated with children could account for women's increased participation in the labor force. That is, it was assumed that if women had less work to do in the household, they would fill their available time with paid labor. Similarly, studies of women's labor force participation have focused on the impact of women's increasing education on their labor force activity. Women with more education will be both more prepared to participate in the paid labor force and more reluctant to forego the economic rewards that their increased education and better jobs can command (Shelton and Firestone, 1988; Blau and Ferber, 1986). In addition to the focus on the changing circumstances of women, there has been some research attention to women's changing attitudes. The women's movement was examined as a source of changes in women's preferences (Evans, 1980). Women influenced by the demands of the women's movement were thought to be more likely to participate in the paid labor force.

To some extent, women's participation in the labor force challenges the notion that there are separate spheres within which men and women exist and work, and that this differentiation is unproblematic (Parsons and Bales, 1955). As such, the increases in women's labor force participation rate led sociologists and family researchers to examine the impact of these shifts on the household. As researchers began to examine the impact of changes in women's participation in the paid labor force on the division of labor in the household, they also began to examine women's labor force participation in more detail. For example, rather than simply focusing on women's labor force participation rate, some scholars began to study women's rate of full-time labor force participation, since some of the increase in women's labor force participation came in the form of part-time work. Thus, some researchers have examined women's paid labor time rather than focusing only on their participation in the paid labor force. There are now numerous studies examining the nature of women's labor force participation, not only in terms of their hours spent in paid labor (Spitze, 1988) but also in terms of occupational segregation (Reskin and Roos, 1987; Barrett, 1979). A number of researchers have also examined the factors associated with women's labor force participation as well as the pattern of labor force participation over women's life-cycles (Goldin, 1989; Lichter and Costanzo, 1987; Rexroat, 1990; Sprague, 1988).

Until quite recently, most of the research on the impact of women's employment on the family focused on the impact of maternal employment on children (Nye, 1963; Powell and Steelman, 1982; Tolman et al., 1989), on marital stability or happiness (Leslie, 1982; Locksley, 1980; Wethington and Kessler, 1989), or on household earnings (Gerstel and Gross, 1989; Oppenheimer, 1982; Sorensen and McLanahan, 1987). In some of this research, there was an implicit assumption that certain pathologies were likely to be associated with women's employment, or at least with married women's employment (Leslie, 1982). More recently, researchers have begun to examine the implication of women's employment, especially married women's employment, for the division of labor in the household and, more generally, for women's and men's gender roles (Pleck, 1985; Shelton, 1990; Smith, 1979).

The study of the links between paid labor and the household has challenged traditional conceptualizations of the family and sex role expectations. Rather than assuming that there is a natural gender differentiation in the household, examination of the links between the labor market and the household requires a conceptualization of the family that is quite different. At a minimum, one has to assume that gender-differentiated roles in the labor market and in the household are not "natural," and that changes in one sphere can influence the other (Blood and Wolfe, 1960).

This focus on the household has required some reevaluation of the nature of activities typically undertaken in the household. Most basically, some household activities are now considered work; thus sociologists now routinely recognize that work may be paid (e.g., work accomplished in the labor market) or unpaid (e.g., work typically accomplished within the household, by a household member). Although the conceptualization of household labor is similar in much of the research, it requires some definition.

For the purposes of this book household labor and housework are terms used interchangeably and refer to a variety of household activities. Although the specifics of my definition and measurement of household labor are described in Chapter 2, some conceptual definition of household labor is necessary at this point. Household labor comprises those activities required for the maintenance of a household and typically accomplished without remuneration. Thus, household labor is distinguished from paid labor because the former is typically unwaged. Household labor also can be characterized as work that is accomplished solely for its concrete results, rather than for what it can bring in trade. Thus, meal preparation in the home is household labor because it is done in order to produce the meal, as distinguished from meal preparation in a restaurant which is done not for the meal per se, but for a wage.

There are a variety of tasks normally considered household labor, including tasks typically done by men (e.g., auto maintenance, outdoor chores) and tasks most often done by women (e.g., meal preparation, indoor cleaning). Although the specifics of measurement of household labor vary among the surveys used for the analyses to be presented in this book, the definition of household labor is the same for all the surveys used.

Although many studies evaluating household labor include childcare in the definition of household labor, it is not included in the definition of household labor in this study. Childcare is certainly household labor, but its measurement is more problematic than is the measurement of other household tasks. Because childcare is excluded from my definition of household labor, the estimates of household labor time in this research will be lower than those estimates including childcare.

A number of perspectives on the division of household labor have emerged in the last thirty years. The resources perspective of Blood and Wolfe (1960) is a classic, but a variety of other approaches to understanding the division of labor in the household have been developed. The resources or power perspective suggests that one's household labor time is a function of one's resources relative to one's spouse's resources. Thus, the spouse with higher socioeconomic resources (e.g., education, income) will have more power and will, therefore, spend less time on household labor (see Ericksen et al., 1979). The relative resources explanation for household labor time relies on the assumption that household labor is onerous so that only those without the power to avoid it will do it (Blumstein and Schwartz, 1991; Coleman, 1991; Perrucci et al., 1978).

An alternative explanation for an association among earnings, education and household labor time is offered by Gary Becker (1975, 1981) and the New Home Economists. Becker (1981) and the New Home Economists also argue that the spouse with more earnings potential will do less housework (and spend more time in paid labor), while the spouse with lower earnings potential will do more housework but less paid work; for them this is an outcome of a rational—and consensual—process (Farkas, 1976). This explanation assumes that the absolute level of household labor (and paid labor) done by husbands and wives, as well as change in household labor time, is rationally determined by the family through deliberate negotiation between spouses. Others have argued that, while the division of household labor may change in response to changes in women's and men's paid work time, the initial level of household labor is not determined by a rational process (Spitze, 1986). Similarly, Sarah Berk (1985) argues that the allocation of resources within the household partially reflects normative expectations of "who should do what."

Some argue that ideology, specifically sex role attitudes, explains the household division of labor between women and men. According to this explanation, men's and women's sex role ideology determines how much household labor they will do; men with traditional sex role attitudes are expected to do less housework than men with non-traditional attitudes (Huber and Spitze, 1983; Ross, 1987). Conversely, women with traditional attitudes are expected to do more housework than women with less traditional attitudes. If men's and women's household labor time is changing, we might then expect sex role attitudes to be associated with the change, rather than accounting for the change in terms of changes in men's and women's resources. In spite of the common observation that there are normative expectations about the accomplishment of household labor that, at a minimum, mediate the impact of resources on household labor time, research findings do not consistently find an association between sex role attitudes and the division of household labor (Coverman, 1985; Geerken and Gove, 1983; Stafford et al., 1977).

More recently, some have argued that, rather than reflecting resources or attitudes, the division of labor in the household reflects time availability (England and Farkas, 1986; Perrucci et al., 1978) or demands and response capability (Coverman, 1985). This explanation suggests that men and women participate in housework and childcare to the extent that they have available time. Shelley Coverman (1985) argues that both time availability and demands affect household labor time. That is, she argues that men will participate in household labor to the extent that there are demands on them to do so. Thus, one would expect women's greater involvement in the paid labor force to be negatively associated with their household labor time but positively associated with other family members' household labor time, specifically husbands' (Ross, 1987). The amount of time that men and women have available is partially determined by paid work time, such that fewer paid work hours mean more response capability, while more paid work hours translate into less response capability (Coverman, 1985; McAllister, 1990). The research regarding the time constraints explanation is inconclusive, with some finding that time constraints and demands affect men's and women's household labor time (Coverman, 1985; Farkas, 1976) while others find no association (Meissner et al., 1975; Model, 1981; Ross, 1987; Szinovacz, 1977; Vanek, 1974).

It is clear that the different perspectives on the determinants of household labor time and the division of household labor all assume that the division of labor within the household is not "natural" but variable and subject to change. Different researchers do, however, identify different forces that may impact on the division of household labor. The current efforts to explain the division of labor in the household differ from the 1950s approach, which assumed that women's roles were expressive, since housework was not seen as work or as instrumental, and men's roles were instrumental and involved financial obligations. They also differ in that women's work in the household is no longer simply classified as expressive; the extent to which it is instrumental is recognized. Thus, researchers now examine what was once taken for granted.

In the research on the connection between changes in women's labor force participation and the household, some see only weak links between the labor market and the household and assert that the shifts in women's labor force participation have not fundamentally altered the household division of labor (Coverman and Sheley, 1986; Shelton, 1990). These researchers may be more inclined to emphasize the impact of normative expectations rather than resources or time constraints (Fenstermaker et al., 1991). Others see stronger links between paid work and unpaid work and argue that women's changing roles in the labor force have led to shifts in gender roles, specifically in the division of household labor (Davis, 1982; Juster, 1985; Pleck, 1985). Some of this disagreement revolves around poor measurement of household labor time as well as differences in the interpretation of small shifts in the division of household labor. In terms of measurement, many studies have included only proportional measures of time use, indicating what proportion of household labor is done by the wife or husband, rather than indicating the absolute amount of time husbands or wives spend on household labor time (Ross, 1987). Other measures include only very approximate estimations of household labor time (Coverman, 1985). These types of measures make it difficult to determine accurately the impact of women's increased labor force participation on the household. For example, when an increase in women's paid labor time is found to be positively associated with men's *share* of household labor, it is impossible to determine whether this shift in men's share of household labor reflects a decrease in women's household labor time or an increase in men's household labor time. In addition, some measures that assess only how much time women and men spend in a broad range of household chores may only poorly reflect actual household labor time (Pleck, 1985).

   In some instances researchers disagree about the significance of observed shifts in the division of household labor, with some interpreting relatively small shifts as significant and indicative of probable future movement (Gershuny and Robinson, 1988; Juster, 1985; Pleck, 1985), with others seeing small shifts as basically insignificant (Coverman and Sheley, 1986; Sanik, 1981). Some of this disagreement results from the conflation of change that is the result of shifts in household composition and change that occurs independently of such shifts. For example, a reduction of average family size may account for some of the reduction in women's household labor time (Robinson, 1977; Shelton and Coverman, 1988). This reduction may be incorrectly attributed to an increase in paid labor time if the change in household composition is not taken into account. Change that exists even after change in household composition has been taken into account may be more correctly attributed to shifts in women's labor force participation rates (Robinson, 1977).

The relative resources, ideology, and time constraints perspectives have been used in attempts to account for the division of household labor in married couple or cohabiting households, rather than simply to explain the household labor time of men and women, whether they are single or married. Even when individuals' housework time is the focus, the explanations generally include some relational measures. For example, women's housework time may partially be accounted for by reference to the gap between their earnings and their husbands' earnings. Similarly, implicit in the hypothesis that women with more egalitarian sex role attitudes will do less housework is the idea that these women will get someone else (e.g., a spouse or partner) to do more housework. This focus has resulted in research that has excluded those who are not married, although a few studies have focused on unmarried cohabitors (Denmark et al., 1985; Yllo, 1978). This is a serious drawback to much of the current research since it is not clear to what extent the division of labor within households and married women's and men's household labor time are functions of the dynamics of the relationship, or to what extent they mirror the household labor time of unattached, unmarried women and men. If men and women do similar amounts of household labor whether they are married or not, then we may see the differences as a function of gender roles. If, on the other hand, the differences between women and men increase with marriage or cohabitation, we can see the differences as at least partially a function of gender roles *within* relationships (Coleman and Walters, 1989).

The time constraints explanation for housework time can be adapted to exclude information on spouses. The household labor time of a person without a spouse or partner may be affected by his or her paid work time in that an employed person may simply spend less time on housework than a non-employed person, even though this decrease may not be accompanied by an increase in a spouse's or partner's housework time. There may simply be less housework accomplished, or substitutes for housework time may be purchased.

In addition, although one's resources relative to other household members may affect household labor time, an individual's earnings may also directly affect household labor time even when there are no other household members present. Earnings may be associated with household labor time if those with higher earnings limit their household labor time because of the greater "costs" of household labor time. That is, the higher one's earnings, the greater the opportunity cost of time spent outside of the labor force.

Finally, sex role attitudes may affect household labor even when no partner or spouse is present. Women with non-traditional sex role attitudes may reduce their household labor time without having a spouse/partner replace it; that is, they may lower their standards. Similarly, men with non-traditional attitudes may spend more time on household labor than men with traditional sex role attitudes even though they are not taking over tasks often performed by a partner/spouse.

Most of the research on women's and men's time use has focused on paid labor and household labor with little attention to the relationship among household work time, paid work time and leisure. There has, however, been some research on the impact of shifts in paid and unpaid work time on the distribution of leisure time (Nock and Kingston, 1989; Shaw, 1985). Increases in women's paid work time, especially if not accompanied by reductions in household labor time, may be associated with decreases in their leisure time (Shaw, 1985; Firestone and Shelton, 1988). The type of leisure in which women engage may also be affected by a redistribution of work time even if total work time (both paid and unpaid) does not increase (Gentry and Doering, 1979). Men's leisure time may be affected by the general trend toward fewer paid work hours (Parker, 1976); they may have more leisure time to the extent that they do not increase their unpaid work time. Finally, women's and men's leisure time expenditures may be interrelated such that any changes in a wife's leisure may affect her husband's and vice versa (Deem, 1986).

The method for defining leisure is more problematic than is the case for household labor time. Shaw (1986) has argued that leisure cannot be objectively defined because it is experienced differently by different individuals. Even if we accept that the definition of leisure must be objective, some activities are more difficult to define than others. For this study, my definition of leisure resembles that of Reuben Grounau (1977). That is, leisure activities are those activities that cannot be enjoyed through a surrogate. Thus, watching television and reading books are defined as leisure activities.

Researchers have found that men have more leisure time than women (Coverman and Sheley, 1986; Shaw, 1985) and that women's household labor time may affect their leisure time, while men's paid labor time affects their leisure time (Clark et al., 1978). In addition, Susan Shaw (1985) reported that employed women have less leisure time than full-time homemakers, suggesting that the dual responsibilities of household labor and paid labor may constrain women's leisure time and that the observed difference between women and men may reflect the dual responsibilities and time commitments of employed women. These findings are consistent with the research reporting an increased workload for women in the paid labor force (Meissner et al., 1975).

Although there are a number of studies examining changes in women's (and men's) paid labor time, the impact of paid labor time on household labor time and, to a lesser extent, the impact of paid labor and household labor on leisure time, there are no systematic examinations of how time expenditures have changed; that is, there are few longitudinal analyses of time expenditures utilizing comparable measures and samples. Of the analyses that do exist there are even fewer that explicitly deal with shifts in paid work time and unpaid work time as distinct but interrelated time expenditures (a notable exception is Pleck, 1985). In addition, there are no comprehensive treatments of the determinants of time use. There are a number of studies that examine the determinants of time use (Berk, 1985; Coverman and Sheley, 1986) and some that examine the trends in time use patterns (Juster, 1985), but no analyses systematically integrate a longitudinal analysis of the changes in time use patterns with an analysis of the determinants of time use and how they may have changed.

WOMEN, MEN AND TIME: A SYNTHETIC ANALYSIS

This book, then, has a double focus. It is a description of change in women's and men's time use and it is an analysis of the factors associated with these patterns. In examining time use, particularly gender differences in it, I focus on the changing (or unchanging) nature of gender roles. Women's and men's time use is examined in detail by focusing on what they do, how much time they spend doing it, and how their time use changed between 1975 and 1987, a period often characterized as one of rapid change in gender roles.

Rather than simply describing women's and men's time use I explore both its individual and structural determinants. To do this I utilize national samples of individuals in order to assess both how women and men spend their time and the personal characteristics associated with various modes of time use. I examine not only how differences between men and women are associated with time use patterns, but also how their characteristics may differently affect their time use patterns. Finally, I assess the extent to which we can understand gendered time use patterns and individual determinants of time use by looking at them within a broader context.

Time Use: Why Study It?

The way people use time tells us something about those people and about the society within which they live. I use this window into people's lives in order to study change. Many have studied and continue to study change by looking at attitudes, but a better indicator, or at least a different indicator, of change is behavior. By utilizing information about time use, we can observe, indirectly at least, how people behave and how their behavior has changed or stayed the same.

In this study time use is categorized into one of three broad categories: paid work time, unpaid work time and leisure. To understand the content of people's lives (or days) we look at their time use patterns. We may see gender differences in how people use time, with men spending more time in paid labor and women spending more time in unpaid labor (Berk, 1985). If we have a starting point, in this instance 1975, we can assess both the nature of change in behavior generally as well as the nature of change in gendered behavior. These changes may indicate convergence, divergence or stability in how women and men spend their time.

Time use can be used as an indicator of gender roles and, as such, the study of change in women's and men's time use is an examination of changes in women's and men's gender roles. In recent years the media have proclaimed the convergence in women's and men's roles, heralding women's entrance into the paid labor force and men's increased involvement with family and domestic life in general (Berman, 1990; New Kind of Life with Father, 1981). Men are not only supposed to be more involved with their families than in the past; they are depicted as doing more housework, just as women are described as doing more paid work. Thus, the media inform us that gender roles are changing so that women's and men's lives are becoming more similar. Women and men are, according to this depiction, no longer confined to their traditional spheres of household and market, respectively, but are free to move between these two spheres.

If this is the case, we might also expect these shifts to be accompanied by changes in the amount of leisure time available and in the gendered pattern of leisure. If men are increasing their domestic labor time, they may be decreasing their leisure time, or at least changing their leisure activities to reflect new constraints on their time. At the same time, to the extent that women's time spent in paid labor and unpaid household labor is changing, we can expect to see shifts in both the amount of time they have for leisure and in the types of leisure activities on which they spend their time.

Looking at individuals' time expenditures is preferable to examining only their attitudes if the goal is to understand how they live. In examining gender roles it is particularly important to use measures of behavior if we want to know about behavior, since some views of gender roles are more "acceptable" than others; respondents may be less traditional in their views than in their behavior (Coverman, 1985; Newcomb, 1983). To the extent to which we are interested in gender roles, we are interested in behavior.

In many instances it is easier to say that we *should* study behavior than to actually study it. Measuring behavior is problematic because we most often have to *ask* people what they do; thus their recollections of behavior are usually confounded with their *views* of appropriate behavior. In this research, data on people's behavior were collected in order to minimize the confounding effect of attitudes. For 1975 and 1981, respondents accounted for their time expenditures during the previous twenty-four-hour period, rather than in general (see Chapter 2 for more details on data collection). These data allow description of both what people do and how much time they spend doing it. The data for 1987 provide less specific measures of time use, but enough specificity to get a reasonably unconfounded measure. Respondents accounted for their time spent on nine specific household tasks. By comparing time use in 1975, 1981 and 1987, we can see how behavior has changed. The information on behavior is made more interesting by the additional information on respondents' attitudes. This allows us empirically to assess the similarity between behaviors and attitudes as well as the effect of attitudes on behavior.

Change in time use may be reflected in shifts in the amount of time spent in paid labor, unpaid labor and leisure, but it may also occur within these broad classifications. Thus, examination of change in time use will focus on that which occurs within paid work, unpaid work and leisure categories as well as on shifts between categories. From 1975 to 1987, for example, there may have been shifts in the types of unpaid household labor performed as well as in the amount of time spent on specific household tasks. These shifts, like shifts in the total amount of unpaid or paid labor, may signal important changes in people's behavior as well as in the gendered pattern of time use (Shelton, 1990). Thus, in this analysis of time use the focus is on both types of change, or the lack of change.

In addition to describing the patterns of change in paid work time, unpaid household labor time and leisure time, this study will also examine the determinants of change. There are three kinds of influencing factors of interest: individual characteristics, household characteristics and other time use.

Time use is influenced by individuals' characteristics such that changes in the latter may produce changes in the former. In this study, I examine the effects of individuals' characteristics on their use of time. In doing so, the sources of shifts in general time use patterns may be uncovered. Changes in the age structure of the United States, for example, may affect the nature of time use if, at the individual level, age is associated with time use. Similarly, educational level may affect individuals' time expenditures. To the extent that these characteristics account for or influence individuals' time use they may affect the general pattern of change in time use. Moreover, if some of these factors influence the time use of women more or less than that of men, changes in them may produce a shift in the gendered pattern of time use, making women's and men's time use more similar (or dissimilar).

Household characteristics may also influence the nature of time use. Individuals' choices about time use are influenced by things other than their own characteristics. The characteristics of other members of their household may also affect time use. An individual's education may influence his or her household labor time, independent of others' education, but it may also have an effect that is the product of the relationship between household members' relative educational levels (Farkas, 1976; Ross, 1987). Thus, a household member's education relative to other household members may affect his or her time use. Other household characteristics also may affect individuals' use of time; the household size may have an effect on each household members' time use. There may be less household labor in small households than in larger ones. Thus, the trend toward smaller households may also be associated with shifts in the general pattern of time use, as well as in individuals' particular time use patterns.

Perhaps more than individual and household characteristics, time use in one sphere is affected by that in other spheres. Time spent in paid labor is time not spent in unpaid work or leisure. Thus, I examine the linkages among paid work time, unpaid work time and leisure time. Time spent in one sphere does not necessarily trade off evenly against time spent in another sphere, just as time spent in household labor may come at the expense of paid work or leisure or both. The tradeoff may also vary by gender such that household labor (or paid work) may mean different types of reductions in other time expenditures for women and men.

The relationship among different types of time expenditures is such that it is impossible to understand an individual's time use in one sphere without reference to his or her other time expenditures. The shift in women's labor force participation from 1975 to 1987 cannot, for example, be understood without reference to their housework time. That is, change in one sphere may make possible or accompany change in the other sphere. In this analysis the focus is on understanding the interconnectedness of various types of time use, making explicit examination of the nature of the relationships among paid work, unpaid household work and leisure necessary. It is impossible to understand women's (or men's) responsibility for household labor without also examining their roles in paid work. In a sense, one makes the other possible.

The entire analysis of time use can be put into a larger context of structures external to individuals and households. Women's primary responsibility for household labor is the result of the devaluation of work performed outside the market. Similarly, men's freedom from most household labor is significant because it means they have more time to invest in "valuable" paid work. This has implications for women's and men's roles and it helps put those roles in a context so that they may be understood as products of forces independent of individuals' motivations or circumstances.

The gendered division of time has implications not only for the relationships between women and men (where men gain power and women lose it) but also for the economy. The gendered use of time both allows the labor force to be reproduced efficiently and it creates an elastic work force. Given these conditions, it is easy to see that women's and men's decisions about their use of time cannot be understood as simply the result of individual or household characteristics or even as the outcome of individual decision making. Individuals make decisions in a context and it is sometimes only possible to understand choices by looking at that context. Educational level is associated with time use for a reason. We may explain it as the product of micro-level processes, but that accounting is incomplete. Instead, education is associated with time use for reasons that cannot be determined by looking at only individual-level variables. That is, we may not be able fully to understand the impact of individual level characteristics on time use unless we also examine the context within which they have an influence.

In addition to context providing insight into time use, we can better understand these invisible structures that are external to individuals and households by looking at time-use patterns. To the extent to which women are subordinated by men, we can understand that subordination by looking at direct measures of behavior. In this book, although time use is examined as an outcome of individual characteristics, household characteristics and time use in other spheres, all of these processes are put in a larger context, thus shedding light on both explanatory variables and time use itself.

Plan of the Book

In Chapter 2 the data and general methodology used in the study are described. Chapter 3 examines women's and men's labor force participation. The chapter focuses not only on participation rates and change in participation rates, but also on trends in men's and women's paid labor time. In addition to presenting basic information on women's and men's paid labor time, the chapter includes an analysis of those individual and household factors associated with women's and men's paid labor time.

Chapter 4 builds on the analyses of Chapter 3 by presenting data on trends in women's and men's household labor time from 1975 to 1987. The impact of personal and household characteristics as well as paid labor time on household labor time is also examined. I focus on presenting the determinants of household labor time and comparing differences between women and men. In addition to examining the patterns of change in total household labor time and the determinants of household labor time in Chapter 4, I also address time spent on specific household tasks. The analysis of specific household tasks provides information on task segregation as well as on time differences between women and men.

Chapter 5 extends some of the analyses in Chapters 3 and 4 by examining the impact of paid labor time and household labor time on leisure time and the types of leisure activities in which women and men engage. Unlike Chapters 3 and 4, Chapter 5 includes data only from 1975 and 1981 because of the unavailability of information on leisure time for 1987. Nevertheless, we can assess the nature of the interconnections among paid work, unpaid household labor and leisure activities.

The final chapter in the book summarizes the empirical information and analyses presented in Chapters 3, 4 and 5. In addition, Chapter 6 focuses on the context within which we can make sense of the empirical findings and goes beyond interpretations that depend simply on the relationships between individual and household characteristics and time use.

2

Methodology

In this study I describe and analyze men's and women's time use and, as such, I examine their time spent in paid work and housework in 1975, 1981 and 1987 and their leisure time in 1975 and 1981. This type of analysis makes it possible to assess both the extent to which there has been change in men's and women's time use patterns and the extent to which men's and women's time use patterns have changed in different ways. Moreover, the book seeks to elucidate the ways in which paid work affects household labor and the ways in which paid work and household labor affect leisure time. Finally, I attempt to determine whether the patterns of time use and the determinants of time use vary depending on the socio-demographic characteristics of individuals. For example, if there is some convergence in men's and women's paid work time, is there more convergence among some respondents than among others? Does paid labor time affect young men's and women's household labor time more or less than it affects older men's and women's household labor time? Does the presence of children affect the pattern of time use for paid work and leisure, and is the effect the same or different for women and men?

In order to begin to assess all of these issues, one must be able to describe time use patterns accurately. That requires access to data that are more or less representative of the United States population, as well as data that include adequate measures of time use. Although there has been some research on changes in time use patterns as well as analyses of the determinants of time use, relatively few studies include uniformly good measures of time use. Moreover, those studies that do have good measures of time use are often based on samples from which one cannot generalize to the United States as a whole.

The analyses presented in this book are based on data collected in two separate studies, both of which are based on representative national samples. The 1975-1981 Time Use Longitudinal Panel Study (Juster et al., 1983) is the source of the data for both 1975-76 and 1980-81. In the Study of Time Use (STU), data were collected from respondents in two separate panels. Respondents provided information on their time use and a variety of other characteristics in 1975-76 and were subsequently recontacted in 1980-81. In both 1975-76 and 1980-81 data on time use were obtained by using time diary measures.

The 1987 data are from the National Survey of Families and Households (NSFH) (Sweet et al., 1988). Estimates of time use in the NSFH are based on questions about average time spent on specific housework tasks. Although not perfectly comparable to the STU data, the NSFH provides relatively good estimates of time use and allows for comparisons across time between the data sets (Marini and Shelton, 1991).

The 1975-76 STU contains data on 1,519 respondents. In both 1975-76 and 1980-81 data were collected in four separate waves. In the 1975-76 panel of the study, 920 of the respondents completed at least three of the four waves of data collection and were eligible for inclusion in the second panel of the study. From the 920 eligible for the second panel (1980-81), data were collected from 620. In the original sample, respondents were selected randomly from a representative sample of U.S. households. In the 1975-76 panel, data for the initial wave were collected via personal interviews, while data collected on subsequent waves were collected through telephone interviews. Similarly, in the 1980-81 panel, in some waves data were collected via personal interviews, while in others telephone interviewing techniques were used (Juster and Stafford, 1985). Although the 1975-76 panel of the STU is a representative sample, there was some attrition between 1975 and 1981. Nevertheless, the samples from 1975-76 and 1980-81 are similar in terms of basic demographic characteristics (Table 2.1).

The NSFH includes data from 13,017 respondents. The main sample includes 9,543 households plus an oversampling of minority respondents, single parents, cohabiting persons, recently married persons and respondents with step-children. The data set is weighted to compensate for the oversampling of these groups. One adult per household was selected randomly to be the primary respondent, and his or her spouse/partner (if applicable) was then the secondary respondent. Portions of the main interview were self-administered. In this study, data on time use were collected by a series of questions about absolute amounts of time spent on various household tasks. The data for the NSFH were collected in one interview, rather than in separate waves. The time use data indicate the average time respondents spend on nine selected household tasks in a week. Previous research has shown that estimates of time use based on direct questions yield higher estimates that those estimates based on time diaries. Nevertheless, because respondents were asked to estimate time spent on separate tasks, these measures may more accurately reflect actual time use than those measures that are based on estimates of total time spent on household labor.

One of the major reasons for using national probability samples as the data base for this research is to provide reasonable estimates of change in time use. While data collected differently (e.g., in qualitative interviews) may more easily lend themselves to interesting explication, data from national samples allow for more valid general statements about time use patterns.

These representative samples each contain high quality measures of time use, although the measures are different. The STU contain data on time use collected from time diaries, while the NSFH measures of time use are derived from direct questions.

In the STU the time diaries were constructed so that respondents accounted for their time for a twenty-four hour period. On the interview day, respondents were asked to account for their time in the previous twenty-four hour period. The diary format was open-ended, with respondents providing information on the beginning and ending times of various activities (see Appendix A for a list of activities). Although the data were collected for a previous day, research has shown relatively high recall when respondents account for their time for the previous twenty-four hour period (Juster and Stafford, 1985). The open-ended question format, while requiring some effort to get information, generally yields more precise estimates of time use than closed-ended diary items and than those with units of measurement specified a priori.

The four waves of data collection in each panel of the STU ensure representation of different seasons as well as different days. In the 1975-76 panel, wave 1 was conducted in the fall, wave 2 in the late winter, wave 3 in the spring and wave 4 in the summer. In the 1980-81 panel data for wave 1 were collected in late winter, wave 2 data in the spring, wave 3 data in the summer and wave 4 data in the fall (Juster and Stafford, 1985: 91). In both 1975-76 and 1980-81, data for two waves were collected for weekend days and two waves were collected for weekdays. The spacing of the waves of data collection throughout the year and the collection of data for both weekend days and weekdays help ensure that the diary estimates are valid indicators of actual patterns of time use.

Only those respondents who completed at least three waves in the original 1975-76 panel were included in the analysis; they were the only ones eligible for inclusion in the 1980-81 followup. To be included in the analyses on the 1980-81 data, respondents must have completed at least three of the four waves of data collection in 1980-81 as well. Thus, for both 1975 and 1981 we can be relatively confident that the measures represent "typical" days. The four individual day measures were transformed into synthetic week measures used in this analysis. The synthetic week measures were calculated by multiplying the individual day accounts by 2.5 (or by five when only one day was available) and adding that to the weekend day time estimates. If only one weekend day was available it was multiplied by 2 before being added to the weekday estimate. These synthetic week measures are better estimates of time use because they are less susceptible to the influence of atypical days than are individual day measures.[1]

Although the time diary data are good indicators of actual time use, a second limitation is that they may underestimate time spent on some activities. For example, time diary estimates are likely to underestimate women's household labor time because respondents are not likely to include small segments of time spent on household tasks. For example, if a respondent spends five minutes straightening the living room, this may be excluded from a retrospective time diary measure. On the other hand, respondents may be less likely to overestimate their "usual" time spent on activities. A second drawback of these measures is the possibility that tasks that occur infrequently but occupy a large block of time may be missed with time diary measures. One would have to collect data on time use for many more days to ensure the inclusion of rare but time-consuming tasks.

The NSFH data contain measures of time use derived from direct questions pertaining to typical time use patterns. Respondents were asked to estimate their time spent in a series of nine housework activities in a week (see Appendix A for a list of activities). Comparisons of direct questions about time use and time diary measures of time use show that estimates of time use using the different methods are similar. Generally, however, estimates of housework time using the direct questions produce higher estimates of time use than do time diary measures. The differences in the estimates of time use using the two methods are, however, generally small; therefore, we can cautiously compare the estimates of time use for 1975-76 and 1980-81 with those of 1987. Since the main purpose of this research is to assess differences in women's and men's time use patterns, the use of direct questions and time diary measures is less problematic than it would be if the purpose were only to estimate absolute changes in time expenditures. In most of our comparisons across different types of measures we calculate the relative contributions of men and women to ensure comparability. When we use absolute measures, some caution should be observed since the direct questions are likely to provide somewhat higher estimates of time use than the time diary measures.

Table 2.1 provides descriptive information on the samples in the 1975-76 STU, the 1980-81 STU and the 1987 NSFH. The data show only small differences in the characteristics of respondents in the three samples. The 1975 and 1981 STU are 43.2% and 40.5% female, while in the NSFH 47.4% of the sample is female. Average age in the three samples is similar, although the average age in the 1981 STU is slightly higher than in the other two samples. Average education is similar in each of the data sets, although NSFH respondents are slightly more likely to be high school graduates, while the 1981 STU has a higher proportion of high school graduates than the 1975 STU. The higher percentage of high school graduates in the 1981 STU reflects some disproportionate attrition of low-education respondents from 1975 to 1981.

There are some differences between the samples as well. The NSFH has a higher proportion of black and other minority respondents, a higher percentage of respondents employed full-time, and more respondents who have never been married. The 1981 STU has fewer respondents with no children than do the other two samples. Although the overall demographic characteristics of the samples are similar, some of the differences may also reflect real changes in the population characteristics rather than sample variability (e.g., employment status, education).

For the most part my analyses are based on information about individuals rather than couples. Analyses conducted only on couples might reveal slightly different patterns than those of individuals; nevertheless, it is important in these analyses to describe individuals' time use rather than only the time use patterns of couples or individuals who are married. In the

Table 2.1
Means, Standard Deviations and Percentages for the Independent Variables Used in the Analysis 1975, 1981 and 1987

	1975	1981	1987
Gender			
Women	43.2%	40.5	47.4
Men	56.8%	59.5	52.6
Age Mean	44.8	48.8	43.4
(Std)	(18.0)	(16.0)	(17.7)
Employment Status			
Not Employed	52.3%	59.2	37.7
Part-time	4.4%	5.0	9.6
Full-time	43.3%	35.8	52.7
Race			
White	89.0%	93.7	80.1
Black	8.5%	4.2	11.1
Other	2.5%	2.1	8.8
Education Mean	11.7	12.6	12.4
(Std)	(3.2)	(3.2)	(3.0)
High School Degree	57.3%	58.7	64.3
College Degree	15.3%	22.4	18.7
Children			
None	55.4%	46.3	56.2
One	14.8%	14.8	17.3
Two or More	29.8%	38.9	26.4
Marital Status			
Married	64.4%	71.9	61.1
Single, Prev. Married	23.1%	24.5	18.2
Never Married	12.5%	3.5	20.7
Number	1,519	620	13,017

multivariate analyses of household labor time I incorporate some information about spouses, but for most of the analyses only information on individuals is used.

STRUCTURE OF ANALYSES

The findings and analysis sections of the book are structured into three main chapters. In Chapter 3 I examine paid work time; in Chapter 4, housework time; in Chapter 5, leisure time. This organization allows me to examine paid work time first and then to incorporate paid work time in determining the factors associated with household labor time. Finally, both paid work time and household labor time are incorporated into the analysis of leisure time. That is, paid work time affects household labor time and both paid work time and household labor time affect leisure time.

In each chapter I first explore the patterns of time use by examining time use in 1975, 1981 and, in Chapters 3 and 4, 1987. Initial descriptions are followed by more specific within-group comparisons. For example, rather than comparing the paid work time of all women and men I compare the paid work time of college educated women and men, or married women and men. Finally, multiple regression is used to evaluate the determinants of paid work time, household labor time and leisure time. Multiple regression analysis (MRA) allows me to evaluate the relative strength of influence of a variety of factors and to determine the source of any observed gender differences in time use. For example, gender differences in household labor time may at least partially be due to gender differences in paid work time. In addition, I determine whether the determinants of time use (for paid work, housework or leisure) vary by gender. For example, I assess whether paid work time affects men's housework time more than women's.

The analyses of household labor time and leisure time require that information on paid work time (and household labor time in the case of leisure time) be included in the analyses. It is clear from previous research that women's and men's time spent in paid labor has an effect on the amount of time they spend on household labor (Berk, 1985; Coverman, 1985), although the size of the effect is less clear. Some research has also shown that the impact of paid labor time on household labor time varies by gender such that women's paid labor time affects their household labor time more than does men's paid labor time affect their household labor time. Thus, although women's and men's household labor time may be a function of a variety of factors, including number of children, education and age, the demands of paid work are an important factor affecting the amount of time available for household labor time. As Coverman (1985) argues, paid labor time can be seen as a constraint affecting one's ability to partici-pate in household labor.

Similarly, both paid labor time and household labor time may determine the amount of time men and women have available for leisure time (Berk and Berk, 1979; Nock and Kingston, 1989; Shank, 1986). In addition, given the differences in women's and men's investments in paid labor and household labor, they may affect women's and men's leisure time differently. Thus, the organization of the book allows me first to assess paid work time and changes in paid work time, followed by an analysis of the impact of paid work time and other individual and household characteristics on household labor time. Finally, in Chapter 5 the effects of paid labor time, household labor time and individual and household characteristics on men's and women's leisure time are examined.

Inasmuch as this analysis examines data for 1975, 1981 and 1987 we also can assess the extent to which change in men's, and particularly women's, labor force participation has affected their household labor time and leisure time. We may examine, for example, whether change in women's paid work time is associated with their leisure time or whether it comes at the expense of household work. Although we cannot explicitly determine the impact of change in one type of time use on other activities, by examining general trends we can get some idea of how time use has been redistributed in response to shifts in women's and men's labor force participation rates and changes in the household division of labor.

The relationships among various general categories of time shed light on the nature of change in that they may indicate changes in the prioritization of types of activities. That women are spending more time in paid work and less time in unpaid household work may signal some reprioritization of these activities. Similarly, in examining shifts within broad categories of time, we can uncover these same types of reordering by looking at what activities command more time and what command less time. We can also see how women and men are changing their time use patterns to reflect some convergence or further divergence in gender roles. This can be observed even if there has been little shift in overall time use patterns. Sometimes the most significant shifts are obscured by looking only at gross patterns of change. For example, we may find that although men's total contribution to household labor has changed little, their relative contribution to meal preparation may have increased as their contribution to outside household tasks has decreased (Shelton, 1990). This type of pattern would indicate some convergence in gender roles in the household, but may be unobservable by looking only at total household labor time.

Finally, it is insufficient to examine only the general patterns of time use change and the relationships among general types of time use. A multitude of individual and household characteristics affect time use. We cannot know, for example, if a decrease in unpaid household work is the result of a deprioritization of this work as such or whether it is the product of a reduction in household size without examining the impact of household size on time use (Robinson, 1977). Similarly, if there has been a general reduction (or increase) in some types of time use, we cannot know exactly who is reducing household time without analyzing individual patterns of time use and the individual- and household-level influences on time use.

In addition to allowing a better understanding of time use, my examination of the individual and household determinants of time use provides information on the characteristics of those individuals with particular time use patterns. Thus, we can see where the changes are occurring, if they are occurring at all. Moreover, even if there are no aggregate changes in time use, time spent on specific tasks may change or there may be increases in some groups' time spent on some activities and decreases in other groups', such that average time spent on paid labor, housework and leisure remain unchanged, even though the time use of some groups changes, or time spent on specific tasks and activities is redistributed.

NOTE

1. My measure of time use includes information only on amount of time and no measure of *when* the time is expended. For example, I have not incorporated information on when a respondent works his/her eight hour shift. Previous research (Nock and Kingston, 1988) has indicated that when time is spent is an important influence on family life, so this limitation should be kept in mind.

3

Labor Force Participation

One of the most visible indicators of change in gender roles is the increase in women's time spent in the labor force. Whereas forty years ago it was somewhat unusual for a woman to be employed outside of the home, and even more unusual for a woman with children to be in the labor force, today the majority of women are in the paid labor force and over half of women with children under the age of six are employed outside the home.

Women's changing roles in the labor force are made more obvious by the increase in the number of women in high profile occupations. Elizabeth Dole's position as Secretary of Labor under Reagan, Geraldine Ferraro's candidacy for the Vice-Presidency, and even the increase in the number of women who are anchors on local news shows attest to the changes in women's labor force activity. This activity is also visible in the frequency with which we encounter women in the paid labor force. One cannot go into a bank or an office without seeing employed women. In addition, women are frequently attorneys in law offices, doctors in hospitals and professors in universities. Thus, the shift is obvious, even if the many ramifications of the change are less obvious. In this chapter I describe women's and men's labor force participation and the individual and household characteristics associated with women's and men's time spent in paid labor. In doing so I assess women's and men's characteristics and the impact of these characteristics on the gender gap in paid labor time.

In 1987 the gap between women's and men's labor force participation rates was about 20%, with women's participation rate at 56% and men's at 76.2% (see Table 3.1). This relatively small gap in participation rates is the smallest ever recorded. If we look at women's and men's labor force participation rates for 1975 and 1981 and compare them to 1987 rates, it is clear that even in that twelve year period there was some convergence in women's and men's labor force participation rates, primarily as a result of the increase in women's labor force participation, but also due to a small decline in men's rate of participation. Women's labor force participation rate was 46.3% in 1975 but increased to 52.1% by 1981 (Table 3.1). During that same time period men's labor force participation rate fell from 77.9% to 77%. This general trend continued to 1987, resulting in further convergence in women's and men's participation in the paid labor force.

As Joseph Pleck (1985) has indicated, these shifts in women's and, to a lesser degree, men's labor force participation rates have implications for how we conceptualize the family. This is due primarily to the perceived impact of women's labor force participation on the family. Family researchers have begun to focus on the extent to which one's earnings or labor force participation are related to one's power within the family, while others have begun to examine the implications of women's dual roles in the labor market and household (Blood and Wolfe, 1960; Meissner et al., 1975). Thus, the changes in women's labor force participation rates have been the subject of research for a number of reasons. First, these changes both indicate changes in the structure of the labor market and foster such changes; second, they may have implications for gender roles in general and the division of labor within the family in particular.

Comparison of women's and men's labor force participation rates does not, however, provide a complete description of their attachment to the labor force. The labor force participation rate

Table 3.1
Participation in the Labor Force by Year: 16 Years of Age and Older (as a Percentage of Non-Institutional Population in the United States)

	Men	Women
1975	77.9	46.3
1981	77.0	52.1
1987	76.2	56.0

Sources: U.S. Bureau of the Census, *Statistical Abstract of the United States: 1989* (109th edition). Washington, DC p. 381
U.S. Bureau of the Census, *Statistical Abstract of the United States: 1982-83.* (103rd edition). Washington, DC p. 377

is calculated by dividing the number of people working or looking for work by the non-institutionalized population age sixteen and older. Thus, the labor force includes employed individuals as well as those who are unemployed but actively looking for work. It also includes individuals employed full-time as well as those employed part-time. As such, the labor force participation rate provides us with partial information about the characteristics of women's and men's activities in the labor force. Of particular importance in this study are the hidden yet systematic differences between women's and men's time spent in the paid labor force that data on the labor force participation rate obscure. Women, for example, are more likely than men to be employed part-time.

Of those in the paid labor force in 1987, 84.2% of men were employed full-time and an additional 5.3% were looking for full-time work, compared to 69.3% of women employed full-time and 4.6% looking for full-time work (Table 3.2). Thus, the 20% gap between men's and women's labor force participation rates

Table 3.2
Percentage of Those in the Paid Labor Force Employed Full-time or Looking for Full-time Work by Gender, 1987

	Men	Women
Employed Full-time	84.2	69.3
Looking for Full-time Work	5.3	4.6

Source: U.S. Bureau of the Census, *Statistical Abstract of the United States: 1989* (109th edition). Washington, DC p. 381.

underestimates the difference between them since men are more likely than women to be employed full-time.

The gender gap in labor force participation also varies depending on which age cohorts are being compared. As Table 3.3 shows, the gap between women's and men's labor force participation rates is generally smaller among younger age cohorts and larger among older age cohorts.

In 1987, among those twenty to twenty-four years of age women's labor force participation rate was 73%, compared to 85.2% for men. This 12% difference is smaller than that for any other age cohort, except for those age sixty-five and older. The similarity between young men's and women's labor force participation rates probably reflects several phenomena. Women and men in this age cohort are less likely to be married or to have children than members of older age cohorts. Single women's labor force participation rates are higher than married women's, and women without children participate more than women with preschool age children (Spitze, 1988; England and Farkas, 1986). The similarity in young men's and women's labor force partici-

Table 3.3
Participation in the Labor Force by Age 1975, 1981 and 1987

Age	1975		1981		1987	
	Men	Women	Men	Women	Men	Women
20-24	84.5	64.1	85.5	69.6	85.2	73.0
25-34	95.2	54.9	94.9	66.7	94.6	72.4
35-44	95.6	55.8	95.4	66.8	94.6	74.5
45-54	92.1	54.6	91.4	61.1	90.7	67.1
55-64	75.6	40.9	70.6	41.4	67.6	42.7
65+	21.6	8.2	18.4	8.0	16.3	7.4

Sources: U.S. Bureau of the Census, Statistical Abstract of the United States:
1989 (109th edition) Washington, DC p. 376.
U.S. Bureau of the Census, Statistical Abstract of the United States: 1982-83
(103rd edition) Washington, DC p. 381.

pation rates may, therefore, reflect family status. In addition, to the extent to which younger women hold more egalitarian attitudes about women working outside the household than older women, we would expect their labor force participation rates to be higher than older women's.

Table 3.3 also shows that women's labor force participation rates increased in every age category except for those age sixty-five or older, from 1975 to 1987. During the same period and in almost every age cohort, men's labor force participation rates declined, although the declines were significantly smaller than the increases that women experienced. For example, among those age twenty-five to thirty-four, women's labor force partic-ipation rate was 54.9% in 1975 but had increased to 72.4% by 1987, while men's labor force participation rate declined from 95.2% to 94.6% during this same period. The most dramatic increase in women's labor force participation rate was for women aged thirty-five to forty-four, whose labor force participation rate increased from 55.8% in 1975 to 74.5% in 1987. Thus, although overall women's labor force participation rate was 56% in 1987, it was significantly higher for some age cohorts. Similarly, men's labor force participation rates were significantly higher among those under age fifty-five than for older men. Nevertheless, for those under age fifty-five, there was significant convergence in women's and men's labor force participation rates from 1975 to 1987. Even with detailed information on women's and men's labor force participation rates, information on time spent in paid labor can provide a more complete description of the nature of their labor force time commitment. So called full-time workers may work forty hours per week or they may work forty-five hours per week. Data on labor force status, even if they include information on part-time and full–time status, do not give us the necessary specificity.

Using 1987 data on time spent in paid labor we see that there is a gap between women's and men's time spent in paid labor (Table 3.4). When considering only those who are employed, on the average men spend 9.2 more hours per week in paid labor than women. Examination of the mean paid labor time for employed women and men reveals that women spend an average of 38.9 hours per week, compared to over 48.1 hours per week for employed men. Thus, although some employed men work less than full-time, men's average paid labor time is significantly more than forty hours per week, while women's average paid labor time is just under forty hours per week. In addition, the size of this gap varies by marital status, number of children, age cohort, and educational level (Tables 3.4 and 3.5).

The gap in paid labor time between unmarried women and men is smaller than the gap between married women and men. Married men spend 10.9 more hours per week in paid labor than do married women, but the gap is only seven hours per week between unmarried women and men (Table 3.4). Phrased differently, married women spend 77.4% as much time in paid labor as

Table 3.4
Hours Spent in Paid Labor for Women and Men by Marital Status and Number of Children, 1987

	Men	Women	Women as a % of Men
Grand Mean	48.1	38.9	80.9
Marital Status			
Married	48.3	37.4	77.4
Not Married	48.7	41.7	85.9
Single Never Married	46.9	43.1	91.9
Cohabiting	49.7	40.7	81.9
Number of Children			
None	46.6	39.8	85.4
One	49.5	38.8	78.4
Two or More	49.8	37.6	75.5

married men, while the figure for unmarried women is 85.9%. Among those who are unmarried there is variation in paid labor time depending on whether they have never been married or are cohabiting but not married. Employed never-married women spend 91.9% as much time in paid labor as employed never-married men, proportionately more than any other women. Cohabiting women spend less time in paid labor than never-married women who do not cohabit, but more time in paid labor than married women. Cohabiting women average 40.7 hours per week in paid labor, compared to 37.4 hours per week for married women and 43.1 hours per week for never-married, non–cohabiting women. Among men, cohabitors spend more time in paid labor than any other category, although the gap between cohabiting and married men is quite small. Comparing cohabiting men's and women's paid labor time, we see that cohabiting women spend 81.9% as much time in paid labor as cohabiting men. The variation in the size of the gap is the result of the differential effect of marital status on women's and men's paid work time. Marital status is only weakly associated with men's paid labor time, although unmarried women spend significantly more time in paid labor than married women. Although cohabiting has some effect on women's paid labor time, they spend almost four more hours per week in paid labor than married women.

The gap between cohabiting and married women's and men's paid labor time indicates that cohabitors are different from married respondents as well as from single non-cohabitors. The differences indicate a pattern similar to the differences between married and unmarried women and men. Cohabiting men spend more time in paid labor than never-married men, while cohabiting women spend less time in paid labor than never-married women. There is no substantive difference between cohabiting and married men's paid labor time, but cohabiting women spend over three more hours per week in paid labor than married women.

These comparisons suggest that, for men, having a wife or a live-in partner is associated with a change in their paid labor time, and that for women there are important differences in the status of wife and cohabitor, at least with respect to labor force activity, although the nature of the change varies. It is conceivable that the differences between men with partners and those without is that single, non-cohabiting men may be more likely to receive other forms of support (e.g., parental financial support). That is, getting a spouse or partner may signify greater financial independence for men. For women, on the other hand, cohabiting may signify greater *dependence* than living alone, but getting married may make women even more financially dependent. Thus, cohabiting and married women are more financially dependent than single women, while the reverse is true for men. In addition to indicating possible tradeoffs between women and men, these findings may reflect other, as yet unexamined, differences between married, single cohabiting and single non-cohabiting women and men. Clearly, marriage represents different things to women and men. These data are consistent with the view that the role of husband involves "breadwinning" while the role of wife is not primarily one of earning money. We will examine the impact of marital status on women's household labor time in Chapter 4.

This interpretation is supported by differences in the impact of children on women's and men's paid work time. The more children women have the less time they spend in paid labor, while for men the opposite is true. Men with children spend about three more hours per week in paid labor than do men with no children, while women with children spend at least one hour less per week in paid labor than women with no children. The different relationships between children and paid labor time for women and for men result in women with no children spending 85.4% as much time in paid labor as men with no children but, among those with two or more children, women spend only 75.5% as much time.

As is the case with marital status, having children clearly involves different kinds of time investments for women and men. Men's "breadwinning" role is increased, while women spend less time in the paid labor force (Gerstel and Gross, 1987). The findings that married and cohabiting men spend more time in paid labor than do single men and that men's paid labor time is positively associated with their number of children suggest that men's ties to spouses/partners or children involve a financial obligation. The data further suggest that women's obligations to spouses/partners and children are not financial, or at least not such that additional hours in paid labor are required. Until we examine women's and men's other time investments (e.g., household labor) we can determine neither whether some of men's other obligations may be reduced with marriage, cohabitation or children, nor whether women's household obligations may increase as their paid labor time decreases.

In addition to family status, women's and men's paid labor time may also vary by other characteristics. Table 3.5 shows that age is associated with both women's and men's paid labor time such that those over age fifty work fewer hours while those under age fifty work more hours per week. Variation in men's and women's paid work time by age results in variation in the gap between their paid work time as well. The largest gap in paid work time is between thirty to thirty-nine year old women and men. During these years men spend between ten and twelve more hours per week in paid labor than women, compared to nine hours a week more for those ages twenty-five to twenty-nine and well under ten hours a week more among those age forty and older. Women work more hours in paid labor when they are between forty-five and fifty years of age, while men's paid work time peaks when they are in their thirties and forties. These differences may reflect, once again, the different impact of having children on women and on men. Women in their prime childrearing years work fewer hours in paid labor, while these years are characterized by more paid work time for men.

Although women in their thirties and early forties work fewer hours than women age forty-five to forty-nine, these data do not indicate that this pattern will continue. The young women in this sample may not decrease their paid labor time as they move into their thirties and forties; instead the changes in women's labor force participation may be reflected in increased paid labor time for employed women in their prime childbearing years (O'Connell, 1990; Smith and Ward, 1984; Waite, 1981). Recent data showing the greatest increases in women's labor force participation for married women with young children also may

Table 3.5
Hours Spent in Paid Labor for Women and Men by Age and Education, 1987

	Men	Women	Women as a % of Men
Age			
25-29	48.4	39.3	81.2
30-34	50.3	40.0	79.5
35-39	49.9	38.5	77.1
40-44	49.3	40.1	81.3
45-49	50.2	41.2	82.1
50-54	45.3	38.1	84.1
55+	42.5	35.4	83.3
Education			
Less Than High School	45.3	37.8	83.4
High School Degree	47.5	39.4	82.9
Some College	48.1	39.2	81.5
College Degree	50.0	40.1	80.2

be reflected in higher average work hours for women in their thirties and early forties.

To the extent to which women increase their paid labor time, we may see decreases in men's paid labor time. At least within households, one member's paid labor time is likely to be affected by other household members' time investments in paid labor (England and Farkas, 1986). An increase in women's paid labor time may allow men to reduce their paid labor time. At the same time, there may be other time use accommodations. I examine these other patterns of time use in Chapters 4 and 5.

The gap between women's and men's paid labor time also varies by educational level such that the gap is smallest among those with less than a high school education, even though education is positively associated with both women's and men's paid labor time. The gap between women's and men's paid labor time is largest for those with a college degree because the variation in paid labor time by educational level is larger for men than for women. There are a variety of possible explanations for this pattern. Hours in paid labor should be higher among better educated women (and men) because education is positively associated with occupational status and wage level (McLaughlin, 1982). It is clear that women's paid labor time is responsive to their wage level such that the more women earn, the more time they spend in paid labor (Firestone and Shelton, 1989; Greenstein, 1989). Better educated men may spend more time in paid labor because of the nature of their occupations; professional occupations demand more time commitment than non-professional ones (Kilty and Richardson, 1985; Moore and Hedges, 1971). Since better educated men are more likely to hold professional positions, this may account for some of the relationship between their education and their paid labor time. The opportunity cost for not participating in the paid labor force also is greater the more one earns. To the extent to which education is positively associated with earnings, men with more education will have more financial incentive to participate in the paid labor force. The same positive association between education and earnings may partially explain the positive association between women's education and their paid labor time. In addition, women with more education may have more egalitarian sex role attitudes; to the extent to which egalitarian attitudes about women's roles are associated with behavior, we would expect these women to spend more time in paid labor than women with more traditional attitudes (Dowdall, 1974; Greenstein, 1986; Stafford et al., 1977; Waite and Stolzenberg, 1976).

Examining data from 1981 and 1975, we can determine the nature of change in paid labor time as well as ascertain whether those factors influencing women's and men's paid labor time in 1987 operated similarly in 1981 and 1975. In both 1975 and 1981, married women worked fewer hours in paid labor than unmarried women, while married men worked more hours than unmarried men (Table 3.6). The gap between married women's and men's paid labor time was over fifteen hours per week in both 1975 and 1981, while the gap between unmarried women's and men's paid labor time was just over six hours per week in 1975 and under five hours per week in 1981. These data show that the influence of marital status on men and women is constant from 1975 to 1987, but that among those who were unmarried the difference between women's and men's paid labor time decreased slightly.

Married women's paid labor time as a percentage of married men's paid labor time went from 65.9% in 1975 to 77.4% in 1987. This pattern is consistent with other data showing that some of the largest recent increases in women's labor force participation have been for married women (Greenberger et al., 1988; Waite, 1981). The greatest increase in women's paid labor time occurred between 1981 and 1987, with relatively stable time investments from 1975 to 1981. The change in married women's paid labor time resulted in a smaller gap between married men's and women's paid labor time in 1987 than in 1975 and 1981.

Among unmarried women and men there was little change in women's paid labor time as a percentage of men's. In 1975 unmarried women spent 85.5% as much time as unmarried men

Table 3.6
Hours Spent in Paid Labor Force for Employed Women and Men
by Marital Status and Number of Children 1975, 1981

	1975			1981		
	Men	Women	Women as a % of Men	Men	Women	Women as a % of Men
Grand Mean	45.6	32.5	71.3	44.8	31.6	70.5
Marital Status						
Married	45.8	30.2	65.9	45.5	29.0	63.7
Not Married	43.5	37.2	85.5	41.3	36.5	88.4
Number of Children						
None	41.7	32.2	77.2	42.9	36.4	84.8
One	43.3	32.4	74.8	48.4	30.3	62.6
Two or More	48.8	32.9	67.4	45.6	28.3	62.1

in paid labor compared to 85.9% in 1987. This slight shift and the much larger convergence in married women's and men's paid labor time indicate that the increases in married women's labor force participation are accompanied by increases in employed married women's paid labor time.

The influence of children on the gap between women's and men's paid labor time is also similar in 1975, 1981 and 1987. The more children men have, the more time they spend in paid labor, while the opposite is true for women. In spite of this similarity, women's paid labor time as a percentage of men's is higher in 1987 than in 1975 when children are in the household as well as when they are not. Among those with no children, women spent 77.2% as much time in paid labor as men in 1975 and 85.4% as much in 1987. Although women with children spent proportionately less time in paid labor than men in all years, the gap decreased from 1975 to 1987. In 1987, among those with two or more children, women spent 75.5% as much time in paid labor as men compared to 67.4% as much time in 1975. Thus, some of the convergence in men's and women's paid labor time represents shifts for those with children, and is not only a function of shifts in the paid labor time of those with no children, or of shifts in the percentage of the respondents with no children. These changes represent an increase in the variability of women's roles, although children continue to define different roles for women and men.

Although age is associated with women's and men's paid labor time in 1975 and 1981, the patterns vary by year and by gender (Table 3.7). In 1975 women between the ages of thirty and fifty-four spent more time in paid labor than older women and than women in their twenties, while in 1981 women's paid labor time was highest for women between the ages of thirty-five and fifty. This variation in the pattern may reflect changes in average childbearing age. To the extent to which women are having children later in life, we would expect the years during which they spend the most time in paid labor to change to reflect this. As women postpone childbearing until their early thirties, the average paid labor time of women in their early thirties may decrease, at least to the extent to which women remain responsible for childcare (Spitze, 1988; Wethington and Kessler, 1989). In 1987, women ages thirty to thirty-four and those ages forty to

Table 3.7
Hours Spent in Paid Labor for Employed Women and Men by Age and Education 1975, 1981

	1975		Women as a % of Men	1981		Women as a % of Men
	Men	Women		Men	Women	
Age						
25-29	45.1	29.8	66.1	49.6	29.1	58.7
30-34	48.6	38.3	78.8	43.8	28.9	66.0
35-39	50.4	33.0	65.5	46.7	39.4	84.4
40-44	48.8	33.4	68.4	46.3	36.6	79.0
45-49	49.0	34.4	70.2	52.8	35.9	68.0
50-54	44.9	39.3	87.5	41.8	24.8	59.3
55+	36.1	24.8	68.7	36.2	24.3	67.1
Education						
Less Than High School	44.3	30.1	68.0	46.7	24.5	52.5
High School Degree	46.4	32.8	70.6	46.9	31.3	66.8
Some College	46.8	33.1	70.7	46.5	33.5	72.0
College Degree	44.7	33.5	74.7	41.6	34.3	82.5

forty-nine spent the most time in paid labor, a pattern that is consistent with the delayed childbearing explanation.

If children represent increased demands on men to participate in the paid labor force, we would expect men's peak years of paid labor time to be later as well. The data from 1975 and 1981 indicate that the paid labor time of men in their early thirties declined from 1975 to 1981, perhaps influenced by a change in the timing of women's childbearing. In 1975 men between the ages of thirty-five and thirty-nine spent the most time in paid labor but by 1981 forty-five to forty-nine year old men spent the most time in paid labor. The pattern was similar in 1987, with thirty to forty-nine year old men spending slightly more time in paid labor than other men. In spite of the variations in paid labor time from 1975 to 1987, within each age cohort women generally spent proportionately more time in paid labor in 1987 than in 1975, although the shifts are largest among those under age thirty and among those age fifty and older. Thus, we see two different patterns here; the peak years of paid labor time shifted slightly from 1975 to 1987 and women's and men's paid labor time converged across all age categories.

The relationship between educational level and women's and men's paid labor time is constant from 1975 to 1987. In all years, those with more education generally spent more time in paid labor than those with less education. Within educational categories, women's paid labor time as a percentage of men's was also higher in 1987 than in 1975. However, there are some variations in the relationship between women's proportionate share of men's paid labor time and education across time. In 1975 and 1981, women's proportionate share of men's paid labor time was higher among those with more education than among those with less education, but in 1987 women with less than a high school degree spent 83.4% as much time in paid labor as similarly educated men, compared to from 80% to 83% for those with more education.

The patterns of paid labor time for women (and men) are consistent with the view that the cost of reduced paid work time is higher among those who are better educated. The positive association between women's education and their paid work time may also reflect differences in attitudes. If better educated women have more egalitarian sex role attitudes (Farkas, 1976; Greenberger et al., 1988; Lopata, 1980), their greater paid work time may reflect these attitudes.

Taken together, the data for 1975, 1981 and 1987 indicate that the patterns of investments in paid labor are similar across all years, but that the average time spent in paid labor has changed. Even taking into consideration the fact that paid labor time was measured differently in 1987 than in 1975 and 1981, it is clear that women's paid labor time increased from 1975 to 1987. In addition, the general finding that women's paid labor time as a percentage of men's paid labor time was higher in 1987 than in 1975 indicates that, compared to men, they increased their paid labor time over the twelve year period. This finding is consistent with other research reporting increases in women's labor force participation (England and Farkas, 1986).

Increases in women's labor force participation rates have been attributed to their higher wage rates. With higher wage rates, the opportunity cost for not participating in the labor force is higher (England and Farkas, 1986; Greenstein, 1989; Waite, 1980). If there are opportunity costs associated with not participating in the paid labor force, there are opportunity costs associated with working fewer hours. At higher wage levels, the costs associated with working fewer hours in paid labor are higher than for those with lower wage rates.

Juanita Firestone and Beth Anne Shelton (1989) show that earnings are associated with women's paid labor time such that women generally spend more time in paid labor the higher their hourly earnings. There is, however, a point at which women seem to use their higher hourly earnings to reduce their total paid work time. Given the usual household demands on women, we can understand this as the wage level at which women will trade off additional earnings for household labor.

MULTIVARIATE ANALYSES

A multivariate analysis can help us better understand men's and women's paid labor time by identifying its determinants as well as by identifying the sources of the gender gap in paid labor time. There are a variety of factors that are thought to influence paid labor time, and in the analyses to follow I assess the impact of these factors on men's and women's paid labor time.

Gender is perhaps most commonly thought to influence paid labor time, but the source of the gender influence is not always clear. For example, observed differences in paid labor time between men and women may be a direct result of gender differences in time investments or they may reflect gender differences in the impact of a number of other variables on paid labor time. For example, the difference in the impact of number of children on men's and women's paid labor time may account for some of the observed gender gap in paid labor time. Using multiple regression we can determine the nature of the association between a variety of personal and household characteristics and paid labor time. MRA also allows us to ascertain the association between paid labor time and age, for example, after taking other factors into consideration. That is, if some of the association between age and paid labor time reflects differences in number of children, the simple bivariate association between age and paid labor time may be the result of number of children. With MRA we can examine the relationship between age and paid labor time after removing the effects of number of children, which allows us to determine whether the observed association accurately reflects the impact of age on paid labor time.

In this section we examine the impact of age, number of children, number of preschool age children, marital status, education and gender on paid labor time, as well as the interaction of gender and each of the other independent variables on paid labor time. By examining the interaction of gender with each of the independent variables I can assess whether the variables affect women's and men's paid labor time in the same way or differently.

Some of the gender difference in paid labor time may be due to the differential impact of children on men's and women's paid labor time, rather than arising directly from gender. Of course, if our earlier analyses are supported in the multivariate analysis and we find that children have a negative effect on women's paid labor time and a positive effect on men's paid labor time, that indicates a certain gender effect. But by identifying the mechanisms through which gender operates we can more fully understand the relationship between gender and paid labor time.

Age and age-squared are included in the equation because I expect the association between age and paid labor time to be curvilinear. That is, I expect paid labor time to increase with age up to a point, but then to begin to decrease with increasing age. Including age and age-squared allows me to both determine whether the association between age and paid labor time is curvilinear and to estimate at *what age* the association between age and paid labor time changes. Given that the bivariate association between age and paid labor time is different for women and men (Table 3.5), I have included an interaction term for age and gender. To calculate an interaction term, I have simply created a new variable that is the product of age and gender. By including the interaction term in the MRA I can determine whether the association between age and paid labor time is different for women and men. If the interaction term is significant, it indicates that the association between age (or another variable) and paid labor time varies by gender.

Marital status is included as an independent variable because I expect to find that paid labor time varies depending on respondents' marital status. Once again, the interaction term for marital status and gender is included in order to determine whether the association between marital status and paid labor time is different for women and men once we have controlled for other variables.

Number of children and number of preschool age children are included because they represent demands. That is, respondents with children may have different demands on them than do respondents without children. Moreover, I expect the demands to vary by age of the children, and especially depending on whether there are preschool age children in the household or not. In the bivariate analyses presented earlier it was clear that the impact of children on paid labor time varies by gender; thus I have included interaction terms for number of children and number of preschool children.

Education is included because those with more education are expected to spend more time in paid labor since the opportunity cost of not doing so is higher for those with more education than is the case for those with less education.

As equation 1 in Table 3.8 shows, surprisingly, gender has no direct impact on paid labor time. This indicates that the previously observed gender effect reflects other measured differences between men and women, or the differential impact of other characteristics on men's and women's paid labor time.

Marital status is positively associated with men's paid labor time; married men spend an average of 3.92 more hours per week on paid labor. The significant negative interaction term indicates that marital status operates differently for women and men. By adding the coefficient for marital status to the coefficient for the interaction term, we can see that married women spend 3.91 *fewer* hours in paid labor than do unmarried women, even after we take number of children, age, and education into account. These findings confirm our earlier conclusion that the gender difference in the meaning of marriage is not merely an artifact of other differences between married and unmarried respondents.

Even if men and women are identical in terms of age, education, and number of children, marital status affects their paid labor time differently. Thus, married women's decreased paid labor time is not merely a function of children being present, but reflects the impact of the status of wife on women. For men, being a husband is also associated with paid labor time, but for men the role of husband is associated with increased paid labor time.

These findings also indicate that children, both total number and the number of preschool age children, are associated differ-

Table 3.8

Regression of Paid Labor Time on Age, Age^2, Education, Total Number of Children in the Household, Number of Children Age 0-4, Marital Status, Gender, Occupational Status and Gender Interaction Terms, 1987

	Equation 1[a]		Equation 2[b]	
Gender[c]	.83	(3.06)[d]	4.14	(3.67)
Marital Status	3.92	(.70)***^^^[e]	.73	(.63)^^^
Marital*Gender	-7.83	(.90)***	-4.13	(.86)***
Total Children in Household	1.39	(.32)***^^^	.29	(.27)^^
Children*Gender	-2.63	(.42)***	-1.18	(.40)**
Children Age 0-4 in Household	.01	(.64)^^^	.04	(.51)^^
Age 0-4*Gender	-6.08	(.86)***	-1.76	(.81)*
Education	.94	(.09)***^^^	.17	(.10)+^
Education*Gender	.33	(.13)**	-.48	(.17)**
Age	1.59	(.10)***^^^	.93	(.12)***^^^
Age*Gender	-.63	(.13)***	-.26	(.18)
Age^2	-.02	(.001)***^^^	-.01	(.001)***^^^
Age^2*Gender	-.008	(.001)***	.003	(.002)
Status	---		.04	(.01)**^^^
Status*Gender	---		.07	(.02)**
Constant	.22	(2.17)	27.82	(2.36)
R^2	.32		.10	
Number	12,627		7,894	

a. All respondents.
b. Employed respondents only.
c. Coded as men=0, women=1.
d. Standard error.
e. Significance levels for women.
Sig. levels for men: *** $p \leq .001$, ** $p \leq .01$, * $p \leq .05$, + $p \leq .1$
Sig. levels for women:^^^ $p \leq .001$, ^^ $p \leq .01$, ^ $p \leq .05$, - $p \leq .1$

ently with men's and women's paid labor time. Total number of children is positively associated with men's paid labor time but negatively associated with women's. For each additional child, men spend 1.39 more hours in paid labor each week. Once again, to calculate the effect for women we add the coefficient for children to the coefficient for the interaction term and find that the impact of each additional child is 1.24 *fewer* hours in paid labor.

The association between number of preschool age children and paid labor time is similar. Men's paid labor time is not affected by the number of preschool age children in the household, but their impact is significant and negative for women. Each additional preschool age child in the household is associated with women spending over six fewer hours in paid labor in a week. If our analysis of the different types of demands children make on women and men is correct, we would expect number of preschool age children to be associated with women's paid labor time, but not with men's. Preschool age children are more demanding of time than older children; thus it is not surprising that the presence of preschool age children is negatively associated with women's paid labor time. We expect to find that they are positively associated with women's household labor time. At the same time, the financial demands of preschool age children are not any larger than those of older children. Thus the fact that the number of preschool age children has little impact on men's paid labor time is not surprising. Like marriage, children represent different demands for women and men. These data support the view that children's demands on men are, or are perceived to be, primarily financial, while their demands on women are for time.

Education is positively associated with both women's and men's paid labor time. Those who are better educated spend more time in paid labor, even after taking other variables into consideration. There is, however a significant difference in the effect of education on men's and women's paid labor time, as evidenced by the significant interaction term for education and gender. For each additional year of education women spend more additional hours in paid labor than do men. The findings with respect to the impact of education on paid labor time are consistent with the view that the opportunity cost of not participating in the paid labor force is positively associated with labor force participation. More education is associated with higher earnings; thus paid labor time may be associated with education because the cost of fewer hours in paid labor is higher for those with more education than it is for those with less education. Although my bivariate analyses of the relationship between education and paid labor time indicated that men's paid labor time is more strongly associated with education than is the case for women, the regression results show that, once other characteristics have been taken into account, the effect of education on paid labor time is significantly greater for women than for men. Both women and men spend more time in paid labor the more education they have, thus supporting my argument that women and men may evaluate their paid labor time at least partially in terms of opportunity costs.

The impact of age on paid labor time is more complicated. The association between age and paid labor time is curvilinear for both women and men. Simple calculus allows me to determine that men's paid labor time generally increases with age up to age thirty-nine, where it begins to decrease, while for women the increase in paid labor time associated with age is less steep than for men, but begins to decline when women are forty years old.[1]

These findings suggest only slight life-cycle differences between women's and men's paid labor time. There are differences in absolute paid labor time, but men's paid labor time peaks at approximately the same time as women's. These similar patterns are seen after number of children and marital status are taken into account, indicating that women's and men's paid labor time is partially a function of number of children, but that age is still differently associated with women's and men's paid labor time, reflecting fundamental differences in women's and men's orientations to the paid labor force. Our equation accounts for 32% of the variation in paid labor time. Thus, although we have not accounted for all of the observed variations in paid labor time, we have explained a significant proportion of the variance.

The MRA clearly shows that the observed differences between women's and men's paid labor time result primarily from differences in the impact of those individuals' characteristics on paid labor time. The differential impact of age on paid labor time indicates that paid labor time is associated with stage in the life-cycle differently for women and men. Each year of age is associated with a larger increase in paid labor time for men than for women, so that the gap between women's and men's paid labor time is greater among older age cohorts than among younger.

Some of the most interesting findings are those pertaining to the impact of marital status and number of children on paid labor time. The multivariate results confirm that family status has a different meaning for men than for women, at least with respect to paid labor time. Even after removing the effects of number of children, education and age, married men spend more time in paid labor than do unmarried men, while the opposite is true for women. Similarly, men with more children spend more time in paid labor than men with fewer or no children, even after the effects of other variables are removed. For women, on the other hand, children are associated with less paid labor time.

These findings illustrate that at least some of the observed gender gap is due to the differential impact of family status on women and men. My data support the view that men act as if family represents a financial demand on them, while women behave differently. In Chapter 4 I examine the relationship between family status and household labor time. If my reasoning is correct, we should find that being married and having children are positively associated with women's household labor time. In the case of men, I expect the association to be nonexistent, but if married men and men with children spend more time on household labor, it may come at the expense of leisure time rather than paid work.

The evaluation of the determinants of women's and men's paid labor time has, thus far, been conducted on all women and men, whether they are in the paid labor force or not. The pattern of influence may, however, be different if we look only at those in the paid labor force. That is, individuals' characteristics may be associated with labor force *participation* and, therefore, with paid labor time for all respondents. Those same characteristics may be differently associated with the paid labor time of those already in the labor force. In equation 2 I examine the impact of education, gender, number of children, age and occupational status on the paid labor time of those in the paid labor force. The findings from equation 2 indicate the impact of the independent variables on paid labor time after removing their possible effect on labor force participation. Occupational status is also included in equation 2 in order to assess its impact on paid labor time. It could not be included in equation 1 because those not in the paid labor force have no occupational status. Once again, I have included an interaction term in order to determine if occupational status affects women's and men's paid labor time differently.

In this model, as in the analysis of all women and men, the effect of gender on paid labor time is not significant, although the size of the coefficient is larger than for all respondents (Table 3.8). This indicates that the observed gender difference in the paid labor time of employed women and men is due either to differences in characteristics or, more likely, to differences in the impact of individuals' characteristics on paid labor time.

The findings with respect to marital status and number of children are similar to those for all respondents considered together, but there are important differences. For employed men, marital status has no significant effect on paid labor time. Marital status' lack of effect on employed men's paid labor time (combined with a significant effect when we examine all men) indicates that married men are more likely to participate in the paid labor force than unmarried men, but that once in the paid labor force married and unmarried men's work hours are not significantly different, after other characteristics are held constant. Among those who are employed, married women spend an average of 3.4 fewer hours per week in paid labor than unmarried women. This difference is substantially the same as the four hour difference I found when examining the effect of marital status on all women's paid labor time. This finding points to another significant difference in the impact of marital status on women's and men's paid labor time. Even among employed women, family status impacts their labor force activity, rather than only affecting the likelihood that they will be employed.

Similarly, neither number of children nor number of preschool age children is significantly associated with men's paid labor time, while both are significantly associated with women's paid labor time. By adding the coefficients for number of children and number of preschool age children to the coefficients for the interaction terms, we can see that number of children in the household and number of preschool age children are negatively associated with women's paid labor time. Among employed women, for each additional preschool age child, women spent almost two fewer hours in paid labor per week while for each additional child they spent approximately one hour less per week in paid labor.

These findings are consistent with my hypothesis that children represent a time demand for women but not for men. Thus, Pleck's (1977) argument that family intrudes on women's labor force activity but not on men's is supported by these findings (see also Ferber, 1982; Fox and Nickols, 1983; Glass, 1988). The lack of any significant effect of number of children on men's paid labor time when we examine only those in the paid labor force, combined with the significant effect when we examine all men, indicates that the presence of children makes it more likely that men will participate in the paid labor force, but has no effect on their paid labor time when they are employed. Married men also are more likely to be employed than are unmarried men, but marital status is not significantly associated with paid labor time for employed men.

For employed women and men, the association between education and paid labor time varies by gender, but the pattern is different than when we examine all women and men. When examining employed men, we find that those with more education spend more time in the paid labor force than do those with less education. For women, however, the association is negative, with educated women spending less time in paid labor than those with less education. Each additional year of education is associated with men spending .17 (10.2 minutes) of an hour more in paid labor, while women spend 18.6 fewer minutes in paid labor for each additional year of education. The differences between equation 1 and equation 2 can be interpreted as indicating that those with more education are more likely to participate in the paid labor force but that, among employed women, those with more education spend less time in paid labor. Since our measure of paid labor time includes time spent at one's second job as well as at one's primary job, work at home and travel time to and from work, my findings do not necessarily indicate that those with more education spend less time at their primary job. Better educated individuals may be less likely to hold a second job or they may spend less time traveling to and from work. Thus, our findings only indicate that better educated respondents spend less time on work-related activities than those with less education.

The association between education and paid labor time in the analysis of all respondents may also reflect the fact that occupational status was excluded from the analysis. To the extent to which those with more education are likely to hold higher status jobs, the positive association between education and paid labor time that I found when not including occupational status may also reflect the positive association between occupational status and paid labor time.

The association between age and employed men's and women's paid labor time is curvilinear. Up to the age of forty-six for men and age forty-seven for women, age is positively associated with paid labor time but after that age is negatively associated with paid labor time. It is interesting to note that while the association between age and paid labor time varies by gender when we examine all women and men, there is no significant gender difference when we include only those who are employed. Among those in the paid labor force, paid labor time peaks significantly later than it does when examining all women and men. This probably indicates that age is associated with labor force partic- ipation such that labor force participation declines after age thirty-nine and after age forty for men and women, respectively, while, among those who continue to be employed, their paid labor time does not begin to decline until women and men are in their late forties.

In my analysis of employed women and men, occupational status is positively associated with men's and women's paid labor time, although the effect is larger for women than for men. The difference in the effect for women and men may indicate greater variability in women's paid work time. The findings with respect to occupational status and paid labor time may also indicate that, once education is controlled, those in higher status occupations spend more time at work, traveling to work and doing office work at home. This finding is consistent with the view that the cost for not working is higher for those in high-status jobs than it is for those in low-status jobs.

The relatively low R^2 for equation 2 is significantly lower than the R^2 for equation 1, which indicates that the variables included in the equations affect labor force *participation* more than paid labor time.

CONCLUSION

We have seen that although women's labor force participation rate has been increasing in recent years, a gap remains between women and men. Moreover, accompanying the increase has been an increase in the amount of time employed women spend in the paid labor force. In spite of the increase in women's paid labor time, and a decrease in men's paid labor time, a significant gap persists between women's and men's paid labor time.

The gender gap in paid labor time is the result of gender differences in the factors associated with paid labor time rather than the product of a direct gender influence. Most significantly, the impacts of stage in the life-cycle and family status are different for women and men. Thus, gender affects paid labor time partially through the differential influence of family status on paid labor time.

The importance of family status in determining women's and men's paid labor time is consistent with the argument that different types of time expenditures are interrelated. In Chapter 4 I further examine this connection between the household and labor market by examining changes in household labor time from 1975 to 1987 as well as the individual and household characteristics associated with household labor time. I also examine the direct effect of paid labor time on women's and men's household labor time. I expect family status to affect household labor time, but to do so differently for women and men, just as it affects men's and women's paid labor time differently.

NOTE

1. To determine at what age the association between age and paid labor time changes one must determine the critical point on the curve. This is done simply with the following formula: $b_1X = b_2X^2$ where b_1 = age and b_2 = age^2. By solving for X, the critical point can be estimated.

4

Housework Time

In the last 20 years there has been a dramatic increase in sociologists' interest in the division of household labor. Those who study family have come to recognize that time spent on housework and the division of household labor between men and women are characteristics of families that help us describe and understand them. This interest in housework reflects two separate changes. Some of the activities that occur in the household are now defined as work, rather than as incidental to any definition of "real" work. Thus, sociologists have redefined work to include both paid and unpaid work. They have also expanded the definition to include housework and childcare (Gauger, 1973; Hill, 1985; Oakley, 1974; Vanek, 1984). A second change, at least as important as the recognition that housework is work, is in the definition of the family. Those who study family have come to recognize that the division of labor normally found within the family is not "necessary" but is instead a product of choice, either through conflict or negotiation. There are still those who characterize families as making decisions, but there is increased attention paid to *individuals* within the household and their divergent interests rather than simply focusing on the family as a unit.

Shifts in women's labor force participation also have fostered interest in how the increased similarity of women's and men's labor force participation may be associated with changes in the household division of labor. Thus, in recent years there have been a number of examinations of the links between women's and men's labor force participation and their household labor time. Sociologists expected that changes in women's labor force participation would be associated with change in the household division of labor such that women would do a smaller proportion of household tasks and men would do a larger proportion. This expectation was based on the presumption that women are responsible for household labor at least partially because they have more time. Thus, as women's available time decreased with their increased labor force participation, sociologists expected their household labor to decrease.

In spite of the interest in housework and childcare, there have been few studies that systematically examine change in women's and men's time investments in housework and childcare. Much of the reason for this is that there are very few sources of data on household labor time, and what measures that are available are not generally comparable. Only since 1960 have systematic data on household labor time been collected, although even after 1960 only a few data sets contain any information on household labor time. This reflects the commonly held view that what goes on in the household is not intrinsically interesting since (1) women do it, (2) it is not in the public sphere, and (3) it is not subject to change through policy.

Those studies that have included some information on household labor time have used a variety of measures. Part of the reason for the variety of measures of household labor time is that there is no commonly accepted method for maximizing both validity and reliability in measures of household labor time. In fact, part of the reason that household labor time has been infrequently studied is that there is no perfect way to measure it. Rather than fostering research to develop good measures of household labor time, this problem has more often been used to justify not studying household labor. The variety of measures of household labor time also have made it difficult to compare the results from different studies, making description of the pattern of change in household labor time difficult.

In this chapter I examine men's and women's household labor time in a number of ways. The chapter begins with a simple analysis of household labor time in 1975, 1981 and 1987. This is followed by a comparison of the household labor time of specific groups of women and men, which allows us to determine whether differences in men's and women's household labor time are due to socio-demographic differences between them. In addition, comparing household labor time within socio-demographic groups makes it possible to determine whether some groups of women and men are more similar in their household labor time than others. For example, we might expect that the gap between men's and women's household labor time will be smaller among younger respondents than among older (Juster, 1985), or between the college educated than between those with only high school educations (Farkas, 1976; LaRossa, 1988; Lopata et al., 1980). Finally, MRA is used to assess simultaneously the impact of individual and household characteristics on household labor time as well as to determine the source of the gender gap in household labor time.

In 1987, among those working in the paid labor force, men did 57% as much household labor as women, compared to 54% and 46% as much in 1981 and 1975 respectively (Table 4.1).

These findings suggest very small shifts in the division of labor between men and women, although they indicate that women continue to spend more time on household labor than do men. If we consider these findings along with those from Tables 3.4 and 3.6, it is clear that this increase in men's proportionate share of household labor time mirrors the increase in women's proportionate share of paid labor time. In spite of the similarities in the patterns, women's proportionate share of men's paid labor time is larger than men's proportionate share of women's household labor time in all years.

Women in 1987 reported doing an average of 38.1 hours of household labor per week, compared to 21.9 hours per week for

Table 4.1
Employed Men's Housework Time as a Percentage of
Employed Women's Housework Time, by Year

	Men's Housework Time as a % of Women's
1987	57%
1981	54%
1975	· 46%

men (Table 4.2).[1] The gap between women's and men's domestic labor time also varies by personal and household characteristics. Married women spend more time in household labor than those who are not married, but marital status has no effect on men's domestic labor time. Married men spend only 52.5% as much time on household labor as married women, but among those who are not married men spend 67.1% as much time as women.

The difference between married women's and men's domestic labor time is greater than between those who are unmarried primarily because married women spend over nine more hours per week on household labor than unmarried women. Married women report spending 41.7 hours per week on household labor while unmarried women spend 32.2 hours per week. The gap between married and unmarried men is insignificant. These findings show that marital status affects women and men differently. For women, being married means spending more time on household labor, while for men being married is not associated with household labor time. Thus, among married respondents,

Table 4.2
Hours Spent in Household Labor for Employed Men and Women by Marital Status, 1987

	Men	Women	Men as a % of Women
Grand Mean	21.9	38.1	57.5
Marital Status			
Married	21.9	41.7	52.5
Unmarried	21.6	32.2	67.1

men do over twenty fewer hours of household labor in a week than women.

The number of children in the household is associated with both women's and men's household labor time but, again, there is more variation for women than for men (Table 4.3). Among those with no children, men do 65.6% as much household labor as women, while for those with one child as well as those with more than one child the percentages are 59.6% and 46.5%, respectively. Thus, although men with children in the household spend more time on domestic labor than those with no children, the impact of children on women's domestic labor time is greater, resulting in a larger gap between women and men with children than between those without children. For those with two or more children, women spend over twenty-seven more hours per week on household tasks than men.

The relationship between number of children and women's and men's domestic labor time indicates that, like marriage, children make different demands on women than on men. As we saw in

Table 4.3
Hours Spent in Household Labor for Employed Men and Women by Number of Children in the Household, 1987

	Men	Women	Men as a % of Women
Number of Children			
None	18.5	28.2	65.6
One	26.1	43.8	59.6
Two or More	23.8	51.2	46.5

Chapter 3, men with children spend more time in paid labor than men with no children, while women with children spend less time in paid labor than women with no children. The shifts in paid labor time and domestic labor time associated with children indicate that women's role in the household and men's in the paid labor force are reinforced when children are present. The responsibility that children represent has quite different implications for women's and men's time use. For both women and men, children impact household labor time more than paid labor time. Men with no children spend an average of 18.5 hours per week on household labor compared to 26.1 for men with one child. In terms of paid labor time, men with no children spend 46.6 hours per week on paid labor compared to 49.5 hours for men with one child. Thus, although the presence of children increases both men's housework and paid labor time, the impact is larger on their household labor time. The impact of children on women's time use is different; for women, having children means spending less time in paid labor. For each additional child women spend about one hour less per week in paid labor. For household labor the largest difference is between women with no children and women with at least one child. Women with one child spend an average of 43.8 hours per week on household labor, compared to 28.2 hours per week for women with no children. Comparing women with one child to those with two or more children, we see that additional children increase women's household labor time by over seven hours per week. Thus, for both women and men, having any children is associated with more household labor time, although the impact on women's household labor time is greater than on men's. The differential impact results in men with children doing proportionately less housework than men with no children. The gender gap is present even with no children, but it is exacerbated by the presence of children in the household.

These findings, combined with the analyses of the impact of marriage and children on paid labor time presented in Chapter 3, illustrate the different demands that marriage and children have on women and men. Marriage and children mean significantly more household labor time for women, while for men they are primarily associated with paid labor time. Thus, a large part of the gender gap is due to differences in women's and men's definition of family "obligations." In spite of the popular press accounts of change in men's family roles, the data show that women still do the majority of household labor and that men with children are more likely to spend extra time in the labor force than at home doing laundry. Family may create *conflicts* for both women and men to the extent to which women want to participate in the paid labor force and men want to spend time in the household. But in 1987 those conflicts appear to be resolved through men remaining primarily in the paid labor force and women responding to household demands.

As LaRossa (1988) argues, there may be other differences between women and men. He argues that there may be some cultural expectation for men with children to spend time in the household but that those men may be "technically present, but functionally absent." That is, in addition to gender differences in time investments, there may be differences in behavior and in attitudes.

Women's and men's household labor time varies by their age as well as by household characteristics (Table 4.4). Younger women and men spend more time on household labor than older women and men. The logical explanation for this is that those who are younger have younger children. Young children are associated with more household labor than older children; hence the variation in household labor time by age cohort may reflect differences in household composition as well.

Once again, although domestic labor time varies by age similarly for women and men, the size of the gap between women's and men's domestic labor time also varies by age. Men under age fifty-five spend proportionately more time on household labor than men who are age fifty-five or older. The largest share of household labor is done by men aged forty to forty-four; these men spend 63.5% as much time on household labor as women. This relatively high proportionate share is due primarily to women's reduced household labor time, but also to a peak in men's household labor time. This pattern is somewhat consistent with the views that younger women and men are shifting the division of household labor more than those who are older as well as with the hypothesis that egalitarian attitudes are responsible for behavioral patterns. However, the youngest men and women have a relatively unequal division of household labor, which suggests that concrete constraints associated with stage in the life-cycle affect women's and men's household labor time (Suitor, 1991; Waite, 1980).

The gap between women's and men's household labor time is associated with level of education (Table 4.4). There is a 20.4 hour gap in household labor time between women and men with less than a high school degree, and this gap declines to 15.5 hours per week for those with a college education. Generally, men's household labor time is curvilinearly associated with their level of education, while women's is negatively associated with level of education. Unlike age, number of children and marital status,

Table 4.4
Hours Spent in Household Labor for Employed Men and Women by Age and Education, 1987

	Men	Women	Men as a % of Women
Age			
25-29	24.7	45.4	54.4
30-34	24.8	41.7	59.5
35-39	21.2	40.0	53.0
40-44	22.6	35.6	63.5
45-49	17.4	31.2	54.0
50-54	18.9	32.8	57.6
55+	16.9	33.6	50.3
Education			
Less Than High School	18.9	39.3	48.1
High School Degree	23.0	39.3	58.5
Some College	22.6	38.8	58.2
College Degree	19.7	35.2	56.0

the variation in the size of the gap between women's and men's household labor time by educational level is the product of the association between both men's and women's education and their household labor time. Men with a high school education spend the most time on household labor, followed by men with some college. Men with a college degree, while spending more time on household labor than men with less than a high school education, do not spend as much time on household labor as men with either a high school degree or those with some college. This may reflect the increasing costs of household labor for college-educated men. That is, their higher earnings may raise the opportunity cost of time spent outside of paid labor. Unlike men, women's education is negatively associated with their household labor time, with college-educated women spending over four fewer hours per week on household labor than women with less than a high school degree. Although the gap between women's and men's contributions to household labor time varies by education, in no instance do men spend even 60% as much time on household labor as women.

Not surprisingly, time spent in the paid labor force is associated with domestic labor time, but the variation is greater for women than for men (Table 4.5). Women who work over thirty hours per week in the paid labor force spend 35.5 hours a week on household labor compared to 49.7 hours for women who are employed fewer hours. Men's paid labor time has less effect on their household labor time; their household labor time averages 21.3 hours per week when they are employed thirty or more hours per week, and 26.5 hours per week for those employed less than thirty hours per week. Thus, men's proportionate share of household labor is higher among those who are employed thirty or more hours per week. This is because women who are employed part-time spend significantly more time on household labor than men who are employed part-time.

Thus far, the findings indicate that when comparing all employed women and men, men spend 57.5% as much time on housework as women, but that this share varies depending on

Table 4.5
Hours Spent in Household Labor for Employed Men and Women
by Paid Labor Time, 1987

	Men	Women	Men as a % of Women
Paid Labor Time			
1-29 Hours	26.5	49.7	53.3
30+ Hours	21.3	35.5	60.0

household and personal characteristics. The gap between women's and men's household labor time is, for example, larger among those who are married than among those who are unmarried, just as it is larger among those with children than among those with no children. These findings illustrate the importance of family status in determining the size of the gender gap in household labor time.

We also find that the gap varies by age and education, with generally a smaller gap between women and men in their forties than between older women and men or between those in their twenties. Better educated women and men also have more equal time investments in household labor than less well educated women and men. Finally, the data indicate that there is less difference between women's and men's household labor time among those who are employed thirty or more hours per week than among those employed fewer hours and that this is primarily due to variation in women's household labor time. In the next section I examine the patterns of women's and men's household labor time in 1975 and 1981 to determine if the patterns are the same as those for 1987.

Comparing the data for 1975 and 1981 to those for 1987, it is clear that there has been some convergence in women's and men's domestic labor time. Among those who were employed, men spent about 46% as much time on household labor as women in 1975 and about 54% as much time in 1981 (Table 4.6). This pattern continued so that in 1987 employed men spent about 57% as much time on housework as women. The reduction in the size of the gap between women's and men's household labor time from

Table 4.6
Hours Spent in Household Labor for Employed Women and Men by Marital Status and Number of Children in the Household 1975, 1981

	1975			1981		
	Men	Women	Men as a % of Women	Men	Women	Men as a % of Women
Grand Mean	10.4	22.4	46.4	11.9	22.1	53.8
Marital Status						
Married	10.7	25.3	42.3	11.7	24.6	47.6
Not Married	7.8	16.7	46.7	13.0	17.2	75.6
Number of Children						
None	10.0	20.8	48.1	11.4	17.8	64.0
One	10.5	22.1	47.5	8.9	21.4	41.6
Two or More	10.7	24.8	43.1	12.8	25.9	49.4

1975 to 1981 primarily reflects a slight increase in men's household labor time, but little change in women's household labor time. Overall, the shift in the size of the gap between women's and men's household labor time has been small.

In 1975 and 1981, women's household labor time varied according to their marital status and number of children in the household. As in 1987, married women spent more time on household labor than unmarried women, and women with children spent more time on household labor than those with no children (Table 4.6). For men, the patterns are not as clear. In 1975, married men's household labor time was higher than unmarried men's, but the difference was smaller than for women. In 1981, there was little difference in the household labor time of married and unmarried men, but married men spent slightly less time on household labor than unmarried men. Nevertheless, for both 1975 and 1981 the gap between men's and women's domestic labor time was larger among those who were married than among those who were unmarried, although the difference between those who were married and those who were unmarried was much larger in 1981 than in 1975. In 1975, married men did 42.3% as much household labor as married women. This had increased to only 47.6% in 1981 (compared to 52.5% in 1987).

Unmarried men did more household labor in 1981 than in 1975 such that among those who were unmarried, men did 75.6% as much household labor as women in 1981, compared to only 46.7% as much in 1975. This convergence in unmarried women's and men's household labor time reflects the significant increase in unmarried men's household labor time. Unmarried men increased their household labor time from 7.8 hours per week in 1975 to thirteen hours per week in 1981. This is the only notable shift in married or unmarried women's and men's household labor time over this six-year period.

The pattern of the influence of children on women's domestic labor time is similar in 1975, 1981 and 1987. The more children there are in the household, the more time women spend on household labor. Men's household labor time does not, however, vary by number of children in the household in 1975 and 1981 (although it does in 1987) (Table 4.6). In 1975, men's household labor time was virtually the same for men with no children as it was for those with one or two or more children, while in 1981 men with two or more children spent slightly more time on household labor than those with no children.[2] Thus, these comparative figures show that children went from having no effect on men's household labor time in 1975 to being positively associated with their household labor time in 1987. In 1981, men with two or more children spent the most time on household labor. This is generally consistent with the view that men have been increasing their time spent with children (Pleck, 1985, 1989; Robinson, 1977), although in these data I have no direct indicators that the increase in household labor time associated with children reflects more time spent with children.

In 1975 and 1981, age is not associated with the gap between women's and men's household labor time, although the gaps between women's and men's household labor time are generally larger in 1975 than in 1981 (Table 4.7). For all but one age category, men spent proportionately less time on household labor in 1975 than in 1981. In addition, men's proportionate share of household labor time was generally higher within age categories in 1987 than in 1981.

Variations in men's share of household labor time by education level in 1975 and 1981 are similar to the pattern for 1987, although, once again, within most educational categories men's proportionate share increased from 1975 to 1987. In both years, men's and women's household labor time was more similar the higher their education. Among those who have attended college, men spent proportionately more time in household labor than did those who had not attended college. The primary source of this similarity is variation in women's household labor time in 1981, although men's household labor time varies moderately by education level. In 1975, there was less association between education and men's proportionate share of household labor than in 1981 or 1987, but the variations were due primarily to the

Table 4.7
Hours Spent in Household Labor for Employed Women and Men by Age and Education 1975, 1981

	1975			1981		
	Men	Women	Men as a % of Women	Men	Women	Men as a % of Women
Age						
25-29	9.8	23.8	41.2	9.8	20.6	47.6
30-34	10.3	21.0	49.0	13.2	25.8	51.2
35-39	9.2	23.0	40.0	12.1	19.4	62.4
40-44	8.0	21.6	37.0	10.1	20.1	50.2
45-49	10.9	23.5	46.4	11.1	21.8	50.9
50-54	11.2	20.9	53.6	13.0	25.6	50.8
55+	12.7	22.7	55.9	12.9	22.2	58.1
Education						
Less Than High School	9.7	22.5	43.1	10.0	27.6	36.2
High School Degree	10.2	22.2	45.9	12.9	22.1	58.4
Some College	10.5	22.6	46.5	11.8	20.7	57.0
College Degree	10.9	23.0	47.4	11.5	20.4	56.4

association between education and men's household labor time. There was less change in men's proportionate share of household labor time within education categories from 1981 to 1987 than from 1975 to 1981. Only in the case of men with less than a high school education did men's share of household labor time increase significantly from 1981 to 1987.

As was the case in 1987, in 1981 and 1975 men and women who spent thirty hours or more per week in the paid labor force spent less time on household labor than those who were employed fewer hours per week, although men's household labor time varied less than women's. Table 4.8 shows that, although men's household labor time varied with their paid labor time in 1975 and 1981, in no instance did they spend even 70% as much time on household labor as women. Among those employed at least thirty hours per week, men spent 60% as much time as women on household labor in 1987, compared to 66.5% in 1981. In 1975, men employed at least thirty hours per week spent only 53.1% as much time on household labor as women. The reduction in the gap between women's and men's household labor time from 1975 to 1981 was the result of an increase in men's household labor time combined with a slight decrease in the domestic labor time of women employed full-time.

The association between women's paid labor time and their household labor time is similar in 1975, 1981 and 1987. Women employed at least thirty hours a week spent less time on household labor than those employed for fewer hours, but they still spent significantly more time than men. For all years, women's household labor time is more strongly associated with their paid labor time than is the case for men.

Among women and men employed less than thirty hours per week, there was no increase in men's proportionate share of household labor from 1975 to 1987. In fact, Tables 4.5 and 4.8 clearly show that in 1987 men spent 53.3% as much time on household labor as women, not significantly different from the 54.5% reported in 1975. Although some of this stability in men's proportionate housework time may reflect differences in measure-

Table 4.8
Hours Spent in Household Labor for Employed Women and Men by Paid Labor Time 1975, 1981

	1975			1981		
	Men	Women	Men as a % of Women	Men	Women	Men as a % of Women
Paid Labor Time						
1-29	15.2	27.9	54.5	16.0	28.2	56.7
30+	9.4	17.7	53.1	10.9	16.4	66.5

ment, the data indicate a lack of any *convergence* among those employed less than thirty hours per week. These data indicate that the slight convergence between women's and men's domestic labor time from 1975 to 1987 reflects changes in women's paid labor time, rather than shifts occurring independently of these changes.

GENDER DIFFERENCES IN TIME SPENT ON SPECIFIC TASKS

Overall, employed men spent 57.5% as much time on household labor as women in 1987, but it is not necessarily the case that men's contributions are equivalent across the variety of household tasks. The data on men's and women's total household labor time indicate some task segregation such that men spend more time in paid labor and women spend more time on household labor. Additional task segregation may, however, be revealed by an examination of men's and women's time spent on specific household tasks.

Table 4.9 shows that there are variations in employed men's relative contributions to specific household tasks. Of course, there are time differences that reflect the different amounts of time that are spent *in total* on particular household tasks, separate from those differences that reflect gender differences in time expenditures. For example, more time is generally spent on meal preparation than on other household tasks, although men's time spent is relatively small compared to women's.

The tasks for which employed women's and men's time expenditures are most different are laundry, meal preparation and house cleaning. Men spend only 24.4% as much time on laundry as women, 30.6% as much time house cleaning and 34.8% as much time as women on meal preparation. Looking at all tasks, there is greater variability in women's time expenditures than in men's. Thus, men's relatively low proportionate share of laundry, meal preparation and house cleaning time reflects women's greater time expenditures more than men's reduced time expenditures. Men spend one hour per week on laundry, 2.2 hours on house cleaning and 3.1 hours on meal preparation, while women spend 4.1 hours per week on laundry and 7.2 and 8.9 hours per week, respectively, on house cleaning and meal preparation. There is also a large gap between men's and women's time spent washing dishes. Men spend 2.3 hours per week washing dishes, while women spend 5.6 hours per week. Thus, for four of our nine tasks, men spend less than 50% as much time as women, and less than 40% as much time for three of these tasks. This finding is consistent with other research indicating that women do a greater variety of household tasks (Schooler et al., 1984).

Although women spend more time than men shopping, paying bills and driving to complete errands, the gaps are smaller. Employed men spend 56.7% as much time as employed women on shopping, a figure that probably reflects changes in men's time spent grocery shopping as well as reductions in women's overall shopping time. Employed women have less time to shop than

Table 4.9
Time Spent on Household Tasks for Employed Men and Women, 1987

	Men	Women	Men as a % of Women
Household Tasks			
Preparing Meals	3.1[a]	8.9	34.8
Washing Dishes	2.3	5.6	41.1
Cleaning House	2.2	7.2	30.6
Outdoor Tasks	4.9	2.2	44.9[b]
Shopping	1.7	3.0	56.7
Washing, Ironing	1.0	4.1	24.4
Paying Bills	1.7	2.0	85.0
Auto Maintenance	2.0	0.4	20.0[b]
Driving	1.2	1.7	70.6

a. Measured in hours per week.
b. Women as a % of men.

those who are not employed; hence, the relatively greater equality in men's and women's shopping time may reflect a variety of factors.

Men spend 70.6% as much time as women driving and 85.0% as much time as women paying bills; therefore, these tasks are the least gender influenced of all the household tasks for which we have data. These tasks also have in common relatively low time expenditures by both women and men, which may be partly responsible for the relative equality between women and men.

Two household tasks are characterized by greater time investments by men than by women. Men spend more time than women on routine outdoor tasks and on auto maintenance, with women spending 44.9% and 20.0% as much time as men, respectively. Men spend almost five hours a week on outdoor tasks compared to about two hours per week for women. The gender division of labor that has women responsible for indoor household tasks and men responsible for outdoor tasks still exists, as evidenced by these data. These data also show that men's traditional responsibility for auto maintenance persists although, of all household tasks, auto maintenance consumes the least time. Men spend two hours per week on auto maintenance compared to less than half an hour for women. Thus, although auto maintenance is not very time consuming, men spend significantly more time on it than women.

Women are more likely to work part-time than men. Thus, some of the gap between women's and men's time spent on specific household tasks may be a function of the gap between women's and men's paid labor time. In Table 4.10 I present data for those in the paid labor force at least forty hours per week. These data are surprisingly similar to the data for all women and men in the labor force, indicating that the gap is not merely the result of women's part-time employment status.

Men's time spent on specific tasks is no different when we examine only those employed at least forty hours per week than it is when we look at all employed men. There are a few differences for women, but they are small. When we examine

Table 4.10
**Time Spent on Household Tasks for Men and Women in the Paid
Labor Force 40 or More Hours per Week, 1987[a]**

	Men	Women	Men as a % of Women
Household Tasks			
Preparing Meals	3.0	8.0	37.5
Washing Dishes	2.3	5.2	44.2
House Cleaning	2.1	6.6	31.8
Outdoor Tasks	4.9	2.1	42.8[b]
Shopping	1.7	2.9	58.6
Washing, Ironing	1.0	3.8	26.3
Paying Bills	1.6	2.0	80.0
Auto Maintenance	2.0	0.4	20.0[b]
Driving	1.2	1.7	70.6

a. Measured in hours per week.
b. Women as a % of men.

only women employed at least forty hours per week, we find that their time spent preparing meals, washing dishes and cleaning house are reduced, but by less than an hour per week. For the other six household tasks, women employed forty hours per week or more do not spend significantly less time than all employed women. Time spent on any single task is reduced by no more than fifty-four minutes per week, and when we combine all tasks, women's household labor time is slightly over two hours per week less than when we examine all employed women.

These data support our other findings that show that women's household labor time is somewhat responsive to their paid labor time, but that the association is weak. The small differences between all employed women's time spent on household tasks and the time women employed full-time spend suggests that women's household labor is necessary labor. That is, regardless of women's paid labor time, there are some household tasks that must be accomplished. Thus, women are unable to adjust their household labor time to their paid work demands because the former is nondiscretionary (see also Record and Starrels, 1990).

An examination of the 1975 and 1981 data on women's and men's time spent on specific household tasks reveals some interesting trends.[3] For most household tasks, there is little shift in men's proportionate share, but there are exceptions (Table 4.11). The gap between women's and men's time spent on meal preparation changed slightly from 1975 to 1987 such that in 1987 men spent 34.8% as much time on meal preparation as women, compared to 20.6% as much time in 1975. There was proportionately more change in the gap between men's and women's time spent washing dishes. Men spent only 13.5% as much time as women washing dishes in 1975, but this increased to 21.6% in 1981 and to 41.1% in 1987. Thus, with respect to meals, there has been more change in meal cleanup than in meal preparation. This finding is consistent with the view that women remain responsible for meals, since it is likely to be the person who cooks, rather than the one responsible for cleanup, who sets the timing for meals. There were also small shifts in men's time spent

Table 4.11
**Time Spent on Household Tasks by Employed Men and Women
1975, 1981**[a]

	1975			1981		
	Men	Women	Men as % of Women	Men	Women	Men as % of Women
Household Tasks						
Preparing Meals	1.3	6.3	20.6	1.8	6.3	28.6
Washing Dishes	.27	2.0	13.5	.41	1.9	21.6
House Cleaning	3.7	5.7	64.9	2.2	4.7	46.8
Outdoor Tasks	2.2	1.3	59.1[b]	3.1	1.1	35.5[b]
Shopping	1.6	2.7	59.3	1.6	3.3	48.5
Washing, Ironing	.11	2.1	5.2	.14	2.0	7.0
Paying Bills	.15	.17	88.2	.34	.17	50.0[b]
Auto Maintenance	.09	.20	45.0	.83	.15	18.1[b]
Driving	1.9	2.7	70.4	2.0	2.2	90.9

a. Measured in hours per week.
b. Women as a percent of men.

on laundry as a percentage of women's time. From 1975 to 1987 men's laundry time as a percentage of women's increased from 5.2% to 24.4%.

We might expect men's increased participation in some tasks to come at the expense of male-typed tasks, but this does not appear to be the case. In all years, men spent more time on outdoor chores than women, and women's time on outdoor chores as a percentage of men's actually declined from 1975 to 1981. There were, however, shifts in men's time spent cleaning house that may partially account for other changes. Men's time spent house cleaning as a percent of women's time declined from 1975 to 1987. In 1975 men spent 64.9% as much time as women house cleaning but this declined to 46.8% in 1981 and even further to 30.6% in 1987. Thus, some of men's increased participation in meal preparation, meal cleanup and laundry may have come at the expense of other household chores, indicating a reprioritization rather than a shift in absolute time investments. There was little change in men's and women's relative time expenditures on shopping, paying bills, auto maintenance and driving. In contrast to the common view that men's time spent shopping, especially for groceries, has increased, these data indicate little change in men's relative contribution to shopping.

The segregation revealed by the data on men's and women's time spent on specific tasks also may indicate more segregation than the data directly reveal. For example, the small amount of time men spend on laundry and ironing is probably spent differently than women's time. Women may, for example, spend a greater percentage of their time ironing (a relatively time-consuming task) than is the case for men. Similarly, men's meal preparation time may be spent differently than women's. Given their relatively low time commitment, men probably spend a greater proportion of their time setting the table or on other relatively minor tasks than they do preparing the main course. A similar division probably exists for auto maintenance, with women spending their few minutes differently than men spend their time. Unfortunately, these data do not provide enough specificity to know exactly what tasks men and women perform, nor whether they are "helping" someone else or responsible for the task.

WOMEN'S EMPLOYMENT STATUS AND MEN'S AND WOMEN'S HOUSEHOLD TASK TIME

We have seen that men's time spent on household tasks is not strongly associated with their paid labor time. Nevertheless, men's time spent on household tasks may be influenced by their wives' or partners' paid labor time. Given that women spend more time than men on household tasks and that employed women have less time to devote to household tasks, women's employment status may be associated with their own household task time as well as with their spouses'/partners' household task time. Moreover, as we have argued previously, there may be variation in time spent on specific household tasks even if there is little variation in total household labor time. In fact, the popular media often characterize men's supposed increase in household labor time as a reaction to their wives' increased paid labor time (Berman, 1990). In this section we examine the impact of women's employment status on their own and their spouses'/partners' time spent on specific household tasks.

Table 4.12 presents adjusted mean times for specific housework tasks by wives' employment status and gender, after controlling for individual and household characteristics associated with time spent on household labor. The statistical controls are included so that we can isolate the effect of women's employment status as they are included in the MRA to isolate the effects of other variables. It is necessary to look at adjusted means because the characteristics of households vary more with women's employment status than with other household characteristics. For example, if there are fewer children in households with employed women, any positive effect of women's employment on men's household task time could be masked by the lower average family size. By controlling for individual and household characteristics,

Table 4.12
Adjusted Mean Time Spent on Household Tasks by Wife's Employment Status and Gender, 1987[a]

| | Wife's Employment Status | | | | | |
| | Men | | | Women | | |
	HM[b]	PT[c]	FT[d]	HM	PT	FT
Preparing Meals	2.0	2.4	3.2***	12.1	10.9	8.6***
Washing Dishes	1.8	2.1	2.8***	7.4	6.9	6.0**
House Cleaning	1.5	1.8	2.5***	11.2	9.0	7.7***
Outdoor Tasks	5.6	5.6	6.1	2.3	2.3	1.8
Shopping	1.6	1.3	1.8**	3.5	4.0	2.9*
Washing, Ironing	.5	.6	1.0***	5.7	4.8	4.6**
Paying Bills	1.4	1.4	1.8	1.7	2.1	1.8
Auto Maintenance	1.6	1.6	2.3**	.1	.3	.3
Driving	1.3	.9	1.4*	2.0	2.4	1.8+

a. Controlling for wife's education, wife's age (for women's time), husband's age (for men's time), husband's education, number of children in the household, and number of preschool age children in the household.
b. HM = Homemaker.
c. PT = Part-time.
d. FT = Full-time.
*** $p \leq .001$, ** $p \leq .01$, * $p \leq .05$

we can remove their confounding effects. The analysis is, of course, conducted only on those respondents who are either married or cohabiting with a partner. The analysis reveals differences in women's time spent on specific household tasks by their employment status as well as differences in men's time spent on specific tasks by their wives' employment status.

Overall, the shifts in women's time expenditures are larger than the shifts for men, although there are shifts in time spent on a variety of household tasks for both women and men. Women who are employed full-time spend 3.5 fewer hours on meal preparation than women who are not employed. Similarly, women employed part-time spend more time on meal preparation than women employed full-time, but less time than those who are not employed.

Men's time spent on meal preparation is significantly associated with wives' employment status; men married to employed women spend more time on meal preparation than men married to full-time homemakers. Nevertheless, their meal preparation time varies less than women's. Men whose wives/partners are employed full-time spend 1.2 more hours per week on meal preparation than men married to full-time homemakers. Thus, the increase in men's meal preparation time when their wives are employed does not fully compensate for the decrease in employed women's time.

Time spent washing dishes and cleaning up after meals is also associated with women's employment status. Women employed full-time spend 1.4 fewer hours per week washing dishes than full-time homemakers. Men's meal cleanup time is associated with their wives' employment status, and almost compensates for the decrease in employed women's meal cleanup time. Men married to women employed full-time spend one more hour per week on meal cleanup than those married to full-time homemakers. In total, men married to women employed full-time spend 2.2 more hours on meal preparation and cleanup than men married to full-time homemakers (compared to 4.9 fewer hours spent by women employed full-time compared to full-time homemakers). In households where women are employed, it is clear that less time is spent on meals by men and women than in households where there is a full-time homemaker. Whether additional time is spent by children or other household help is not clear from these data.

Time spent house cleaning is also affected by women's employment status and, once again, women's time is more strongly affected than men's. While women employed full-time spend 3.5 fewer hours on house cleaning per week than full-time homemakers, men married to women employed full-time spend only one more hour per week on house cleaning (8.6 minutes per day) than men married to full-time homemakers.

Women who are employed full-time spend about half an hour less per week shopping than full-time homemakers. Women employed part-time spend more time shopping than either women employed full-time or full-time homemakers. This may reflect the fact that they are "out of the house" more than full-time homemakers, and that they have more discretionary time than women employed full-time. The association between men's time spent shopping and their wives' employment status is opposite the effect for women. Men married to women employed full-time spend more time shopping than men married to full-time homemakers, but men married to women employed part-time spend less time shopping than men whose wives are employed full-time or are full-time homemakers. Thus, men married to women employed part-time do not pick up some of the shopping but leave even more of the shopping to their wives than do men married to full-time homemakers.

Time spent on laundry is associated with women's employment status. Employed women spend less time on laundry than full-time homemakers, and some of this decrease is picked up by husbands/partners. Men whose wives are employed full-time spend half an hour more per week on laundry than men married to full-time homemakers, while women employed full-time spend 1.1 fewer hours per week on laundry than full-time homemakers. Once again, men and women together spend less time on laundry in those households where the woman is employed full-time.

Men's time spent on auto maintenance is associated with their wives' employment status. Men with wives who are employed full-time spend more time on auto maintenance than men whose wives are full-time homemakers or employed part-time. This may reflect these men's reduced hours in paid labor, since it is not an example of men picking up some household work from their employed wives. Women's time spent on auto maintenance is negligible no matter what their employment status.

Time spent driving household members is associated with women's employment status. Men married to women employed part-time spend less time driving other household members than do men married to full-time homemakers or to women employed full-time. As expected, women employed part-time spend *more* time driving other household members than other women. Thus, as is the case with shopping, there is a net redistribution of driving tasks to women when they are employed part-time.

Neither men's nor women's time spent on outdoor tasks or paying bills is associated with women's employment status. Men spend significantly more time than women on outdoor tasks across all categories of women's employment status and women generally spend more time paying bills than do men, no matter what their employment status.

In spite of the significant associations between women's employment status and their own and their husbands' time spent on household tasks, for most household tasks, as well as for the most time consuming household tasks, women spend significantly more time than men. For example, employed women spend at least five more hours on meal preparation in a week than men and at least three more hours washing dishes than men.

SOURCES OF VARIATION IN DOMESTIC LABOR TIME

Thus far, my analysis of household labor time has focused on differences in men's and women's time investments and on variations in household labor time and the gender gap in household labor time. My initial analyses suggest that some personal and household characteristics may be associated with men's and women's household labor time and that the nature of those associations may vary significantly by gender. These findings are consistent with previous research in that they show variation in men's and women's household labor time and that some of the major factors associated with household labor time appear to represent other demands or constraints on time.

There are a variety of explanations that have been offered to account for both the variation in men's and women's household labor time and the gender gap in household labor time. In accounting for individuals' household labor time, the explanation most supported by the data is variously referred to as time availability (Perrucci et al., 1978), demand/response capability (Coverman, 1985) or situational view (England and Farkas, 1986). The time availability explanation accounts for variation in household labor time in terms of different demands and constraints on time. That is, household demands (e.g., children) are associated with increased household labor time but this increase is affected by other demands (or constraints) that may limit one's ability to respond to household demands. Thus, paid employment may act as a constraint on time and limit one's ability to respond to household demands.

In my simple bivariate analyses of the patterns of variation in household labor time, factors associated with demands were found to be associated with women's and men's household labor time. In this section I further examine the time constraints explanation by evaluating the impact of household demands and paid work demands on women's and men's household labor time. This analysis is superior to the bivariate analyses performed thus far because it allows me to examine the impact of demands on women's and men's household labor time after other characteristics have been taken into account. Moreover, I can determine if observed differences in the impact of demands on women's and men's household labor time are statistically significant.

Multivariate Analysis of Determinants of Household Labor Time

A multivariate analysis of the determinants of household labor time will allow me to identify the sources of variation in women's and men's household labor time as well as to better understand the sources of the gender gap in household labor time. One of the major issues I need to address is to what extent the gap between women's and men's household labor time is a function of their differential investments in paid labor time and to what extent the gap remains even after taking their paid labor time into account.

It is commonly known, for example, that women spend more time in household labor than men, whether they are employed outside the home or not. Employed women spend less time in paid labor than employed men and it is not clear to what extent the gap between employed women's and men's household labor time is a function of the gap in their paid labor time. Moreover, in estimating paid labor time, sociologists have generally not included time spent on both a primary and a secondary job as well as travel time to work and work at home. To the extent to which paid labor time impinges on women's and men's ability to spend time on household labor, travel time to work and work at home should affect household labor time as well. Thus, in the analyses to follow, I use a comprehensive measure of paid labor time in assessing its impact on household labor time. I also assess the impact of a variety of other individual and household characteristics on household labor time in order to determine the nature of their effect on household labor time as well as whether there are gender differences in the nature or size of the effects of individual and household characteristics on household labor time.

Marital status, number of children, and number of children under age five as well as gender interaction terms for each of these variables are included as independent variables. In the bivariate analyses marital status and number of children were associated with men's and women's household labor time and the associations were different for women and men. Marital status should be associated with household labor time but I expect a significant interaction term because marital status should be positively associated with women's household labor time but negatively associated with men's. Similarly, I expect the demands of children on men and women to be different; number of children and number of children under age five should be more strongly associated with women's household labor time since our bivariate analyses indicate that women with children spend significantly more time on household labor than women without children.

To the extent to which the opportunity cost for not participating in the paid labor force is higher for those with more education, I expect to find that education will be negatively associated with household labor time for both women and men. Similarly, occupational status may be negatively associated with household labor time because the opportunity costs associated with household labor time rather than paid labor time should be higher for those with higher status occupations. Moreover, the higher one's occupational status, the more power one may have to avoid household labor.

Paid labor time is included as an independent variable because the more time respondents spend in paid labor, the less time they should have for household labor. In addition, since women are more likely to be responsible for household labor, I expect the association between paid labor time and household labor time to be stronger for women than for men.

Finally, age may be associated with household labor time to the extent to which it is associated with the timing of major life course events. There are likely to be gender differences in the timing of these events; thus I have included gender interaction terms to identify gender differences in the association between age and household labor time. The multivariate analyses also allow examination of the impact of each independent variable on household labor time after removing the confounding effects of other variables.

Table 4.13 presents results of the regression of household labor time on selected personal and household characteristics. Equation 1 reveals that after personal and household characteristics have been taken into account, gender has no significant direct effect on household labor time. That is, the observed gender gap in men's and women's household labor time is a function of either (1) differences in their characteristics or (2) differences in the impact of their characteristics on household labor time. This does not indicate that gender is unrelated to household labor time, but only that the effect is not direct. This finding is important, especially when interpreted in light of my earlier findings which showed that women spend more time on household labor than men. This multivariate analysis allows me to investigate the sources of the gap, rather than simply noting its existence.

In addition to investigating the direct effects of gender on household labor time, I examine the effect of the interaction between gender and the other independent variables on household labor time. Finding a significant interaction effect would indicate that gender is associated with the way some other variables affect household labor time. Significant interaction effects would further show that at least some of the observed gender gap in household labor time is due to gender differences in the impact of personal and household characteristics on women's and men's household labor time.

Marital status is negatively associated with men's household labor time; this means that even after holding other variables constant, married men spend less time on household labor than unmarried men. The significant positive interaction term for marital status and gender indicates that the effect of marital status on household labor time is significantly different for women and men. To determine the size of the marital status coefficient for women, I add the coefficient for the interaction term to the coefficient for marital status. In this case, I add 7.39 to -2.04 and find that, whereas for men marital status is negatively associated with household labor time, for women marital status is positively associated with household labor time. Married women spend over

Table 4.13

Regression of Household Labor Time on Age, Education, Total Number of Children, Number of Children Age 0-4, Respondent's Paid Labor Time, Marital Status, Occupational Status, Gender and Gender Interaction Effects, 1987

	Equation 1[a]		Equation 2[b]	
Gender[c]	6.06	$(4.25)^d$	15.10	$(6.30)**$
Marital Status	-2.04	$(.96)*^{\wedge\wedge\wedge c}$	-1.33	$(1.02)^{\wedge\wedge\wedge}$
Marital*Gender	7.39	$(1.24)***$	4.81	$(1.42)***$
Total Children in Household	1.15	$(.44)**^{\wedge\wedge\wedge}$	.81	$(.45)+^{\wedge\wedge\wedge}$
Children*Gender	4.09	$(.61)***$	4.96	$(.70)***$
Children Age 0-4 in Household	.89	$(.86)^{\wedge\wedge\wedge}$	.22	$(.82)^{\wedge\wedge\wedge}$
Age 0-4*Gender	3.06	$(1.20)**$	3.30	$(1.34)**$
Education	.04	$(.12)^{\wedge\wedge\wedge}$	.01	(.17)
Education*Gender	-.86	$(.18)***$	-.42	(.28)
Age	.17	$(.13)^{\wedge\wedge\wedge}$	.03	(.02)
Age*Gender	.52	$(.18)**$	-.29	(.31)
Age^2	-.002	$(.001)^{\wedge\wedge\wedge}$	-.001	(.002)-
Age^2*Gender	-.005	$(.002)**$	.006	(.004)+
Paid Labor Time	-.08	$(.02)***^{\wedge\wedge\wedge}$	-.005	(.02)
Paid*Gender	-.05	$(.02)*$	.04	(.04)
Occupational Status	——		-.06	$(.02)*^{\wedge\wedge\wedge}$
Occupational Status*Gender	——		-.11	$(.04)**$
Constant	19.75	(3.0)	22.23	(3.97)
R^2	.16		.14	
Number	8,831		5,656	

a. All respondents.
b. Employed respondents only.
c. Coded as Men=0, Women=1.
d. Standard error.
e. Significance levels for women.
Signif. levels for men: *** $p \le .001$, ** $p \le .01$, * $p \le .05$, + $p \le .1$
Signif. levels for women: $^{\wedge\wedge\wedge}$ $p \le .001$, $^{\wedge\wedge}$ $p \le .01$, $^{\wedge}$ $p \le .05$, - $p \le .1$

five more hours per week on household labor than unmarried women, while married men spend two *fewer* hours on household labor than unmarried men. The opposite effect of marital status on men's and women's household labor time is consistent with my earlier interpretation of the effect of marital status on paid labor time. These results, combined with the earlier finding of a positive effect of marital status on men's paid labor time and a negative effect on women's paid labor time, indicate that married women are more responsible for the non-financial maintenance of the family, while married men are more responsible for financial maintenance, as evidenced by their greater paid labor time and reduced household labor time.

Number of children is positively correlated with both men's and women's household labor time. For each additional child in the household men spend over an hour more on household labor per week. The significant interaction term for number of children and gender indicates that children represent significantly more work for women than for men. Women spend over five more hours on household labor for each additional child in the household. Thus, if we hold all other factors constant, the demands of children affect both women's and men's household labor time, although the effect is significantly larger for women.

In addition, the number of preschool age children is significantly associated with women's household labor time but not with men's. For women, having a preschool age child in the household is associated with them spending 3.95 more hours per week on household labor. This effect exists after taking total number of children into account. Women's additional household labor time associated with preschool age children, combined with the lack of any association for men, may indicate that the type of household labor associated with children is different for women and men. The findings indicate that the type of labor associated with young children is that which is done predominantly by women.

These findings with respect to the impact of children on men's and women's household labor time support my claim that children, like marriage, represent different types of demands on women and men. As I showed in Chapter 3, having children is associated with men spending significantly more time in paid labor, thus indicating that they are at least perceived as representing financial demands. For women, my results support my claim that children make demands on women's time at home, rather than financial demands. In contrast, children are associated with only very small increases in men's household labor time.

Although education is not significantly associated with men's household labor time, it is negatively associated with women's household labor time. Thus, holding all things constant, better educated women spend less time on household labor than less well educated women. This is consistent with my finding that better educated women spend more time in paid labor. To the extent to which time spent in household labor may come at the expense of other activities (including work related leisure) it is not surprising that better educated women seek to avoid these costs.

Age is not associated with men's household labor time, but it is significantly associated with women's. The positive sign on age and the negative sign on age-squared indicate that the association is curvilinear. Simple calculations reveal that the nature of the association is such that up to age forty-nine, each additional year is associated with more household labor time, but after age forty-nine age is negatively associated with household labor time. These results probably reflect a variety of factors. The positive sign on age may indicate cohort differences in women's household labor time. Older women may have a different view of their household responsibilities than younger women. The shift in direction at age forty-nine may reflect a reduction in household demands associated with aging (e.g., children leaving home, death of a spouse). The lack of any effect for men is not consistent with my earlier finding that young men spend more time on household labor than older men. The bivariate association may reflect greater household demands among young men, rather than actual age effects.

Paid work time is negatively associated with both women's and men's household labor time, although the effect is larger for women than for men. For each additional hour men spend in paid labor they spend 4.8 minutes less on household labor, while for women each hour in paid labor time is associated with 7.8 fewer minutes of household labor. Thus, although the association between paid labor time and household labor time is stronger for women than for men, there is not a one-for-one tradeoff for either men or women. This may indicate that time adjustments are made among a larger number of activities. For example, paid labor may come, at least partially, at the expense of leisure time rather than only household labor time. The larger effect for women indicates a stronger association between women's paid labor time and their household labor time than exists for men. To some extent, this may reflect the greater flexibility in the timing of men's household labor time. We might see this because men do different household tasks than women, in addition to spending less time on them. In addition, these findings indicate that the less time women spend in paid labor, the more time they spend on household labor (while the association for men is weaker). Thus, men are less likely to use available time for housework than are women.

Overall, I have accounted for 16% of the variation in household labor time. These findings indicate that, although I have identified a variety of factors associated with household labor time, others affect it.

Equation 2 in Table 4.13 is run only on those who are employed and includes occupational status as an independent variable. The results are similar to the results for *all* women and men, but there are some notable differences. Among those who are employed, gender is associated with household labor time even after other characteristics have been taken into account. Women spend an average of 15.1 more hours per week on household labor than do men. The significant gender effect here is indicative of employed women's "double day" with responsibility for both paid labor and household labor.

When including only those who are employed, marital status is associated with women's but not with men's household labor time. Married women spend 3.48 more hours per week on household labor than women who are not married. Similarly, children are positively associated with employed women's household labor time. For each additional child women spend almost six more hours per week on household labor, compared to less than one more hour per week for men. The number of preschool children is not associated with employed men's household labor time but they are associated with women's. Each preschool age child in the household is associated with women spending 3.52 more hours per week on household labor. Thus, even for those who are employed, preschool age children represent different sorts of demands on women and men.

Neither age nor paid labor time is associated with employed women's and men's household labor time, although both were associated with household labor time in the equation for all women and men. Occupational status is, however, associated with both women's and men's household labor time, although the effect of occupational status on household labor time is larger for women than for men. The higher the respondents' occupational status, the less time they spend on household labor. This finding is consistent with the opportunity cost explanation. The higher the occupational status, the greater is the opportunity cost for spending time on household labor (rather than in the paid labor force).

The equation for employed women and men explains 14% of the variation in household labor time. Thus, although we have accounted for some of the variation in household labor time, much more remains unexplained.

Thus far I have been examining individuals and the way that their characteristics are associated with household labor time. While individuals' characteristics may be sufficient to account for the household labor time of unmarried respondents, household characteristics and spouses'/partners' characteristics may help account for the household labor time of married or cohabiting respondents (see Nock and Kingston, 1988). For example, we would expect husbands' household labor time to affect wives' household labor time to the extent to which any household labor time done by the husband does not have to be done by the wife.

In the next section of this chapter I examine married and cohabiting women's and men's household labor time by incorporating not only their own characteristics but the characteristics of their spouses/partners as well. My focus only on individuals' characteristics may account for the relatively low explained variance thus far. In examining the determinants of household labor time for married and cohabiting women and men a variety of perspectives can guide the selection of variables. In addition to the time constraints perspective previously outlined, there are two other explanations. With respect to married and cohabiting individuals, the time constraints explanation focuses on the impact of both respondents' and spouses' time demands and constraints on respondents' household labor time. Constraints are generally measured by paid labor time, with those spending more time in paid labor having more constraints on their time. Time demands are measured by number of children, spouse's/partner's paid labor time and spouse's/partner's household labor time. To the extent to which an individual has more children he/she may have more demands to participate in household labor. In addition, the more time one's spouse/partner spends in paid labor, the more demands there may be on the respondent to participate in household labor. Similarly, the more time other household members spend on household labor, the fewer demands there may be on respondents to do so.

In addition to time constraints, household labor time, specifically the distribution of household labor time within married and cohabiting couple households, may be affected by the relative resources of household members. The relative resources explanation seeks to account for the distribution of household labor within households by measuring the resources that women and men bring into the household. Rather than examining only individuals' resources, the focus is on spouses' resources relative to one another. Thus, to the extent to which husbands have higher earnings than their wives, one would expect the former to spend less time on household labor than the latter. The argument is that household members can use their resources to avoid unpleasant or undervalued labor, specifically household labor. If this explanation is correct, one could explain women's greater average time spent in household labor as a product of their lower average earnings relative to their spouses. Another resource that individuals may have is education. The partner with more education may use that resource to avoid household labor. This explanation assumes that resources are power and that the distribution of household labor is a product of a power struggle of sorts between household members, usually between husbands and wives.

An alternative interpretation of the hypothesized relationship between one's resources and one's household labor time is posited by the New Home Economists (Becker, 1981, 1985). New Home Economists argue that, to the extent to which the partner with more resources spends less time on household labor, it is a result of a consensual decision-making process within the household which recognizes that the costs of doing household labor are higher for the partner/spouse with more resources. Given these higher costs, New Home Economists argue that the household decides to have the partner/spouse with fewer resources take responsibility for more household labor. This decision rule is seen as rational for all household members.

The problem with the consensual decision-making postulated by the New Home Economists is that there is evidence that household members disagree about the distribution of household tasks (Blumstein and Schwartz, 1983). In addition, New Home Economists assume that the time spent doing household labor necessarily comes at the expense of paid labor time, thus costing the household money. In fact, research shows that leisure time is often sacrificed to household labor (Nock and Kingston, 1989; Shaw, 1985) so that the costs in terms of paid labor time are not as great, or as direct, as the New Home Economists assume.

Finally, some argue that household labor time is partially a function of ideology such that women with more egalitarian sex role attitudes are expected to spend less time on household labor than those with more traditional attitudes. At the same time, men with more egalitarian attitudes are expected to spend *more* time on household labor that those with more traditional attitudes. There is some research supporting the view that women's sex role attitudes affect their own household labor time (Beckman and Houser, 1979; Koopman-Boyden and Abbott, 1985) as well as some which finds that men's attitudes affect their household labor time (Huber and Spitze, 1983; Perrucci et al., 1978). Other researchers have, however, found either no association between sex role attitudes and household labor time (Rubin, 1976) or that those with more liberal sex role attitudes are more traditional in their use of time than those with more conservative sex role attitudes (Coverman, 1985). This last finding may indicate that an inequitable distribution of household labor leads women to expect household chores to be shared. This expectation may be reflected in sex role attitude measures to the extent to which they include attitudes about the division of household labor. Thus, women's double day is viewed as affecting their attitudes about how household labor should be divided such that women with more responsibilities will be more likely to hold egalitarian attitudes or to feel that household labor should be shared than is the case for women with fewer demands on their time.

I examine these three explanations for household labor time by focusing only on married and cohabiting couples and measuring the extent to which relative resources, time availability and ideology account for women's and men's investments in household labor. When looking at households rather than individuals, I acknowledge that the decisions about time use are not made in isolation but may be affected by other members of the household, in this case by spouses/partners.

What these perspectives do not address, however, are the differences in the household labor time of unmarried women and men. Clearly, those differences are not a result of some interactive process with a spouse but may, instead, reflect differences in sex role socialization or cleaning standards (which reflect sex role socialization).

The Determinants of Married and Cohabiting Women's and Men's Household Labor Time

When I examine only cohabiting or married respondents and incorporate spouses'/partners' characteristics into my analyses I am able to account for more of the variation in household labor time. Equation 1 in Table 4.14 shows that time constraints are among the most important determinants of household labor time but that sex role ideology also accounts for some of the variation in women's and men's household labor time.

Again, although gender has no direct effect on household labor time, there are observable differences in the effects of household and personal characteristics on women's and men's household labor time. Total number of children in the household is positively associated with men's household labor time. For each additional child in the household, men spend almost two more hours in paid labor per week. Total number of children also has an effect on women's household labor time but, as indicated by the significant interaction term, the effect is different for women than for men. Among women, each additional child in the household is associated with an additional 4.59 hours of housework per week.

Number of children under the age of five is associated with women's household labor time but not with men's. For women, each additional child age four or younger is associated with women spending 4.33 more hours per week on household labor. This finding supports our earlier assertion that women and men do different kinds of work associated with children.

Additional time constraints that have an effect on women's and men's household labor time include respondents' paid labor time and spouses' paid labor time. The more time both women and men spend in paid labor, the less time they spend on household labor, although the association between paid labor and household

Table 4.14
Regression of Household Labor Time on Age, Education, Total Number of Children, Number of Children Age 0-4, Respondent's Paid Labor Time, Spouse's Paid Labor Time, Sex Role Attitudes, Gap in Total Earnings, Spouse's Household Labor Time, Gender and Gender Interaction Effects, 1987

	Equation 1[a]		Equation 2[b]	
Gender[c]	4.62	(8.59)[d]	5.66	(9.15)
Total Children	1.97	(.55)***^^^[e]	1.37	(.58)*^^^
Children*Gender	2.62	(.83)**	3.40	(.87)***
Children Age 0-4	.09	(1.01)^^^	-.55	(1.06)^^^
Age 0-4*Gender	4.24	(1.55)**	4.61	(1.57)**
Paid Labor Time	-.10	(.03)***^^^	-.06	(.03)*^^^
Paid*Gender	-.08	(.04)*	-.12	(.04)**
Spouse's Paid Labor Time	.10	(.03)***	.13	(.03)***^^
Spouses's Paid*Gender	.03	(.04)	-.04	(.05)
Sex Role Attitude	-1.44	(.59)*^^^	-1.35	(.64)*^^^
Attitude*Gender	3.58	(.89)***	3.59	(.95)***
Gap in Earnings	-.00	(.00)	-.00	(.00)
Gap*Gender	-.00	(.00)	-.00	(.00)
Education	-.16	(.17)^^^	-.33	(.18)+^^^
Education*Gender	-1.18	(.30)***	-1.12	(.31)***
Age	-.18	(.23)	-.23	(.24)
Age*Gender	.42	(.34)	.37	(.37)
Age^2	.001	(.002)	.001	(.003)
Age^2*Gender	-.002	(.004)	-.001	(.004)
Spouses's Household Labor Time	____		.06	(.02)**^^
Constant	31.87	(6.17)	29.46	(6.68)
R^2	.20		.27	
Number	3,619		2,433	

a. All married or cohabiting respondents.
b. Married or cohabiting respondents with data on spouses' household labor time.
c. Coded as men=0, women=1.
d. Standard error.
e. Significance levels for women.
Sig. levels for men: *** $p \le .001$, ** $p \le .01$, * $p \le .05$, + $p \le .1$
Sig. levels for women: ^^^ $p \le .001$, ^^ $p \le .01$, ^ $p \le .05$, - $p \le .1$

labor is greater for women than for men. For each additional hour men spend on paid labor they spend six fewer minutes on household labor. The impact of paid labor time on women's household labor time is slightly stronger, with women spending 10.8 fewer minutes on household labor for each hour they spend in the paid labor force. Thus, although neither men nor women equally trade off paid work against household labor, the tradeoff is slightly more equal for women than for men. This indicates a more direct relationship between paid labor and household labor for women than for men.

A time demand associated similarly with women's and men's household labor time is spouses' paid labor time. For both women and men, the more time one's spouse spends in paid labor the more time one spends on household labor. For each additional hour a spouse spends in paid labor, respondents spend six more minutes on household labor. This finding is consistent with the view that a spouse's/partner's time in paid labor represents a demand on respondents to participate in household labor. There are, of course, constraints that may limit a respondent's ability to respond to this demand (e.g., paid labor time), but to some extent respondents respond to these demands much as they respond to the demands that children represent.

The sex role ideology explanation for the division of household labor is somewhat supported by these analyses. Men with more conservative sex role attitudes spend less time on household labor than men with more liberal sex role attitudes. Among women, the association is the reverse, as indicated by the significant and differently signed interaction term. Women with traditional sex role attitudes spend more time on household labor than women with liberal sex role attitudes. These findings are consistent with the ideology explanation.

Education is associated with women's household labor time but not with men's. The more education women have the less time they spend on household labor. For each additional year of education, women spend 1.34 fewer hours on household labor. This finding is consistent with the view that the costs of participating in household labor are higher for women with more education and that this additional cost discourages them from spending time on household labor. It may also indicate that women with more education have the resources to resist household labor.

The relative resources explanation is not consistently supported by the analyses presented in Table 4.14. The size of the earnings gap between spouses/partners is not associated with either men's or women's household labor time. I also find that age is not associated with household labor time when I include only married or cohabiting respondents in the analysis. This may indicate that age is a determinant of the household labor time of those without partners but not those with partners. Equation 1 explains only 20% of the variation in household labor time, indicating that a number of other factors are associated with household labor time.

Equation 2 shows that if I add spouses' household labor time to the equation, the results are substantively equivalent, even though respondents' household labor time is affected by his or her partners'/spouses' household labor time. Spouses'/partners' household labor time is positively associated with respondents' household labor time. The time constraints perspective on household labor time would predict that a spouse's/partner's household labor time would be negatively associated with the respondent's household labor time. The logic behind this would be that the less time a spouse/partner spends on household labor, the greater will be the demands on the respondent to spend time on household labor. My results are not consistent with this explanation but rather suggest that when there are demands on one spouse/partner to participate in household labor, there are demands on the other.

Equation 2 does account for more of the variation in household labor time. Thus, spouses'/partners' household labor time contributes significantly to explaining variation in respondents' household labor time, indicating the importance of incorporating data on couples when trying to assess the behavior of individuals who are in couples.

CONCLUSION

We have seen that, although there were changes in women's and men's household labor time from 1975 to 1987, significant gaps in their time investments in the household remain. Women continue to spend significantly more time on household labor than men, although men's household labor time increased slightly from 1975 to 1987, especially when measured as a proportionate share of women's time. Some of the improvement in men's proportionate share of household labor time is the result of decreases in women's household labor time and cannot be attributed solely, or even mostly, to increases in men's household labor time.[4]

In spite of some changes in household labor time, it is significant that family obligations continue to intrude in different ways on men's and women's time. Getting married and having children affect women's household labor time far more than they affect men's. These differential effects can partially account for the gap between women's and men's household labor time. The gender gap in total household labor time is mirrored by a gap between men's and women's time spent on specific household tasks. Women continue to be responsible for meal preparation, meal cleanup and house cleaning while men spend more time on outdoor tasks (see also Record and Starrels, 1990). The gender gap in time expenditures is accompanied by significant task segregation as well.

Overall, we can see that the observed increase in women's labor force participation as well as the increase in their paid labor time is not accompanied by a commensurate decrease in women's household labor time. At the same time, the decrease that we see in women's household labor time is not completely compensated by an increase in men's household labor time.

Chapters 3 and 4 suggest that the shifts in women's time spent in paid labor reflect an increase in women's total work time. This double day, combined with the lack of a double day for men, may have implications for women's and men's leisure time. In Chapter 5 I examine changes in women's and men's leisure time from 1975 to 1981 and assess the impact of paid labor time and household labor time, as well as total work time, on women's and men's leisure time.

NOTES

1. These estimates are based on self-reports of average time spent per day in nine household activities. Research has shown that respondents tend to overestimate their household labor time when asked to report it in this way, but that women and men overestimate equally, making estimates of proportionate shares reliable. When comparing the 1987 data on household labor time to the data for 1975 and 1981, it is important to take into consideration the fact that the 1975 and 1981 data are based on time diary accounts and will, therefore, not represent overestimates like the 1987 data. Comparison of proportionate measures is the best way to assess change.

2. So few men have only one child that no confidence can be placed in the estimate of their household labor time.

3. Comparison of men's household time as a percentage of women's (or, in a few instances, women's as a percentage of men's) allows us to look at the data over time. Estimates of actual time spent on tasks are not comparable because of the differences in measurement between the 1975 and 1981 time diary measures of household labor time and the 1987 measures of household labor time.

4. Michael Lamb (1987) contains cross-cultural comparisons of fathers' roles that reveal significant variations in fathers' roles. Moreover, the research supports Ralph LaRossa's (1988) finding that the ideal norms regarding fathers' roles may differ significantly from the empirical norms.

5

Leisure

The research on women's and men's time use has focused on their paid work and housework time to the almost total exclusion of leisure time. Although there is a large body of literature examining leisure activities (Moore and Hedges, 1971; Tinsley and Johnson, 1984), only a few researchers have examined differences between women's and men's leisure time and even fewer have studied the impact of paid work and household labor on leisure time (for exceptions see Campbell, 1978; Deem, 1982; Shaw, 1985). Those who have studied women's so-called double day imply that there are "costs" to combining paid work and household labor for women, but rarely are these costs discussed in terms of leisure time. At the same time, men's limited involvement in household labor has implications for their leisure time that are rarely examined.

In this chapter I examine women's and men's leisure time in 1975 and 1981. Data on leisure are not available for 1987. In the first section, I examine the patterns of men's and women's leisure time, looking at both time expenditures and particular types of leisure activities. In the second section I evaluate the determinants of leisure time, focusing on the impact of paid labor and household labor time on both total leisure time and on specific types of leisure activities.

In 1981 men spent an average of 36.9 hours per week on leisure activities compared to 37.7 hours per week for women (Table 5.1). The forty-eight minute difference between women's and men's total leisure time may reflect a variety of differences between them, including differences in labor force status, but it is not statistically significant. Table 5.1 also includes average leisure time for employed women and men. A comparison of employed women's and men's leisure time reveals that employed men have 1.6 more hours of leisure per week than employed women. Thus, although women's average paid work time is less than men's, they report slightly less time spent on leisure than men. Among those who are not employed men spend significantly more time on leisure than do women, a pattern that most likely reflects differences in their housework time. This pattern indicates the need to examine leisure time and its determinants more closely.

Table 5.1
Hours Spent on Leisure by Employment Status and Gender, 1981

	Men	Women	Gap Between Men and Women
All	36.9 (15.7)	37.7 (15.2)	-.8
Employed	33.2 (12.7)	31.6 (11.8)	1.6
Not Employed	53.7 (17.3)	45.7 (15.5)	8.0***

*** $p \leq .001$

Table 5.2 includes the leisure time of employed women and men. Women's leisure time varies little by marital status, with married women spending only slightly less time on leisure activities than unmarried women. For men, however, marital status is strongly associated with leisure time. Unmarried men spend over four more hours per week on leisure than married men. This is consistent with the findings in Chapter 3 which show that married men spend more time in paid labor than unmarried men. The additional paid labor appears to come at least partly at the expense of leisure.

Married men's reduced leisure time does not merely reflect more time spent at home, since my measure of leisure time includes leisure activities done in the home (e.g., relaxing, watching television). At this point in the analysis, it is impossible to determine if marital status is associated with type of leisure activity.

Number of children is associated with both women's and men's leisure time, but the pattern of the effect varies. Men with children spend less time on leisure activities than men without children. This finding is consistent with the association between marital status and men's leisure time. I found earlier that family obligations are associated with men spending more time in paid labor. Thus it is not surprising that being married and having children are negatively associated with leisure time.[1]

Women with one child have more leisure time than women with no children and than women with two or more children. This pattern may reflect differences in time demands, with childless women spending more time in paid labor (Table 3.6). At the same time, women with two or more children in the household spend more time on household labor than other women (Table 4.6) and this may come at the expense of their leisure time (Bollman et al., 1975).

Table 5.3 shows that men's and women's leisure time varies with age but that the association between age and leisure time also varies by gender. Men spend the least time on leisure when they are in their forties, while women's leisure time is lowest

Table 5.2
Hours Spent on Leisure for Employed Men and Women by Marital Status and Number of Children, 1981

	Men	Women	Gap Between Men and Women
Grand Mean	33.2	31.6	
Marital Status			
Married	32.5	31.9	.6
Unmarried	36.6	32.1	4.5
Number of Children			
None	35.5	31.7	3.8
One	31.5	34.5	-3.0
Two or More	31.8	30.9	.9

when they are in their thirties. This pattern may reflect the timing of demands on women and men. In 1981, men's time in paid labor was high when they were in their forties while women's household labor time was high for women in their thirties (Table 3.7). Thus, the different timing of paid labor and housework demands on men and women may account for the different patterns of their leisure time.

The gap between women's and men's leisure time also varies by age. For those in their 30s, women have less leisure time than men, but for all other age categories women's leisure time is either equal to or greater than men's, although the differences are generally small.

Table 5.3
Hours Spent on Leisure for Employed Men and Women by Age and Education, 1981

	Men	Women	Gap Between Men and Women
Age			
25-29	32.8	35.8	-3.0
30-34	33.9	27.9	6.0
35-39	33.3	27.2	6.1
40-44	32.2	33.7	-1.5
45-49	30.4	31.9	-1.5
50-54	33.1	33.0	.1
55+	35.4	36.2	-.8
Education			
Less Than High School	31.5	33.2	-1.7
High School Degree	32.4	32.8	-.4
Some College	32.3	30.5	1.8
College Degree	34.7	30.3	4.4

Both women's and men's leisure time varies by their educational level, but the pattern is different for women than for men. Men with more education generally spend more time on leisure than men with less education, but for women those with more education spend less time on leisure. Among those with less than a high school degree, women have 1.7 more hours of leisure per week than men, while for those with college degrees women spend 4.4 fewer hours on leisure than men.

These different patterns may reflect gender differences in the impact of education on other types of time use. In 1981, better educated women spent more time on paid labor and less time on household labor than less well educated women, but their total work time (household labor and paid labor) was greater than that of less well educated women. College-educated women's leisure time may reflect this greater total work load. In contrast, college-educated men spent less time in paid labor than less well educated men, and they spent slightly more time on household labor, but total work time was lower among better educated men. Thus, we can presume that college-educated men's leisure time reflects their reduced total work time.

Some of the patterns of leisure time for 1975 are similar to those for 1981, although some are different.[2] Women report 1.7 more hours of leisure per week than men (Table 5.4). Among those who were employed, there was no difference between women's and men's leisure time. Thus, the impact of employment on men's and women's leisure time is similar, although the pattern of change in employed respondents' leisure time varies by gender. From 1975 to 1981 employed women's leisure time increased, and relative to men their position improved. Among those who were not employed, men had significantly more leisure time than women in a pattern similar to 1981.

In 1975 as in 1981, married respondents spent less time on leisure than unmarried respondents and the impact of marital status was greater for men than for women (Table 5.5). Among those who were unmarried, men spent significantly more time on leisure, while married women's and men's leisure time expendi-

Table 5.4
Hours Spent on Leisure Time by Employment Status and Gender, 1975

	Men	Women	Gap Between Men and Women
All	36.1	37.8	-1.7
	(16.7)	(14.7)	
Employed	31.1	30.6	.5
	(11.5)	(11.6)	
Not Employed	57.9	44.8	13.1***
	(18.5)	(14.3)	

*** p ≤ .001

tures were similar. Unmarried men spent 5.5 more hours on leisure per week than married men, while unmarried women spend 1.2 more hours per week on leisure than married women.

The impact of children on leisure time is similar. The more children respondents have, the less time they spend on leisure. Thus, for both women and men, those who are married and those with children have less leisure time than unmarried and childless respondents. As in 1981, children have a greater effect on men's leisure time than on women's. The greater association between men's family obligations (marital status and number of children) may reflect the greater paid work time of married men and men with children.

In 1975 the gap between men's and women's leisure time within age cohorts is generally more similar than 1981, although only among those in their early thirties do women have significantly less leisure time than men (Table 5.6).

Table 5.5
Hours Spent on Leisure for Employed Men and Women by Marital Status and Number of Children, 1975

	Men	Women	Gap Between Men and Women
Grand Mean	31.1	30.6	
Marital Status			
Married	30.6	30.2	.4
Unmarried	36.1	31.4	4.7
Number of Children			
None	34.3	32.4	1.9
One	29.8	30.8	-1.0
Two or More	28.4	28.1	.3

The association between education and leisure time is similar for women in 1975 and 1981, but different for men. In both 1975 and 1981, women with more education had less leisure time, while for men education was negatively associated with leisure time in 1975, but positively associated with leisure time in 1981. These different patterns in men's leisure time may reflect shifts in the prioritization of leisure and its availability among those with college educations. In Chapter 3 we saw that education was positively associated with paid labor time in 1975, but that in 1981 men with college degrees spent less time in paid labor than men with less education. This shift in paid labor time may account

Table 5.6
**Hours Spent on Leisure for Employed Men and Women by Age
and Education, 1975**

	Men	Women	Gap Between Men and Women
Age			
25-29	31.6	30.9	.7
30-34	30.1	26.2	3.9
35-39	28.2	30.6	-2.4
40-44	31.5	31.8	-.3
45-49	30.8	31.0	-.2
50-54	29.9	29.6	.3
55+	34.3	33.4	.9
Education			
Less Than High School	33.9	31.5	2.4
High School Degree	30.9	30.9	0
Some College	28.8	29.4	-.6
College Degree	30.7	29.2	1.5

for the change in the association of education with leisure time between 1975 and 1981.

TIME SPENT ON SPECIFIC LEISURE ACTIVITIES

Although there are some differences between men's and women's total leisure time, the overall similarity may mask differences in time spent on specific leisure activities. Table 5.7 presents data on men's and women's time spent on specific leisure activities, broken down by employment status.

The differences between men's and women's total leisure time are small, but there are some differences in their time expenditures for specific leisure activities. Among those who are employed as well as those who are not employed, men spend significantly more time watching television and listening to the radio and more time on sports activities than women. Women, on the other hand, spend significantly more time than men socializing outside of the home (e.g., attending movies, concerts, dancing).

Employed men spent an average of twelve hours per week watching television and listening to the radio, while employed women spent only 10.6 hours per week on these activities. Among those who were not employed, both women and men spent more time watching television and listening to the radio than men and women who were employed, but the impact of employment status is greater for men than for women.

Employed men spent 3.8 hours per week on sports activities compared to 1.2 hours per week for women. Time spent on sports activities did not vary by employment status for either women or men. Employed men spent an average of 3.8 hours per week on sports activities compared to 3.6 hours per week for those who are not employed. Similarly, employed women spend 1.2 hours per week on sports activities compared to 1.4 hours per week for women who are not employed.

Table 5.7
Hours Spent on Leisure Activities by Employment Status and Gender, 1981

| | Employed | | | Not Employed | | | | |
	Men	Women	t-test[a]	Men	Women	t-test[b]	t-test[c]	t-test[d]
TV/Radio	12.0 (8.0)	10.6 (7.8)	1.7+	25.9 (18.3)	17.4 (12.0)	2.7**	4.5***	5.6***
Read	3.8 (4.7)	3.4 (3.8)	.9	6.8 (5.8)	5.5 (6.0)	1.1	3.0***	3.5***
Hobbies/ Games	1.4 (2.5)	1.7 (3.4)	1.8	.9 (2.0)	4.3 (6.9)	6.2***	.6	3.9***
Organiza- tions	1.0 (3.7)	.9 (2.6)	.7	3.0 (9.2)	1.6 (4.1)	1.3	1.3	1.8+
Relaxing	.4 (1.1)	.5 (1.5)	-.3	1.1 (2.2)	.6 (1.4)	1.7+	3.3**	.6
Sports	3.8 (5.6)	1.2 (2.0)	5.8***	3.6 (6.7)	1.4 (3.4)	1.9*	-.3	.6
Religion	1.4 (3.1)	1.6 (3.0)	-.6	2.1 (4.8)	2.6 (4.4)	-.6	1.5	2.3*
Spectator Sports	.7 (2.1)	.5 (1.7)	1.0	.4 (1.9)	.3 (1.2)	.4	-1.1	1.1
Social- izing	6.2 (5.8)	8.4 (7.3)	-3.1***	5.5 (6.7)	8.1 (7.4)	-2.0*	-.6	.3
Talking	2.4 (2.6)	2.6 (2.8)	-.7	2.4 (3.4)	3.0 (3.3)	-.9	0.0	1.1

a. T-test for difference between employed men and women
b. T-test for difference between not employed men and women
c. T-test for difference between not employed and employed men
d. T-test for difference between not employed and employed women
+ p ≤ .10, * p ≤ .05, ** p ≤ .01, *** p ≤ .001

In much the same way, time spent socializing outside the household is not strongly associated with employment status; women spent significantly more time than men when comparing those who were employed as well as those who were not employed. Employed women spent 8.4 hours per week socializing while women who were not employed spent 8.1 hours per week. Thus, even though women who were not employed should have had more time for socializing outside of the household than those who were employed, they did not do so. The same association exists for men. Employed men spent 6.2 hours per week socializing compared to 5.5 hours for men who were not employed. Employed women and men may spend more time socializing because they already spend more time outside of the household. For example, some of this socializing may occur at the end of the workday. To the extent that this is the pattern, it is not surprising that those who are not employed spend less time socializing than those who are employed. This pattern may also reflect different kinds of demands on those who are not employed. If household demands dictate that one must be available at home, then those who are not employed may be less able than those who are employed to leave the household for planned social activities.

Employed women and men spent similar amounts of time on hobbies although, among those who are not employed, women spent 4.3 hours on hobbies compared to .9 of an hour for men. In addition, employment status significantly affects women's time spent on hobbies, while it has no significant effect for men. These data indicate that men who are not employed may use much of their extra time watching television while women are more likely to spend time on hobbies.

In addition to gender differences in leisure activities, Table 5.7 reveals that those who are not employed are much more likely to use their extra time to watch television and/or listen to the radio than they are to increase their time spent on other leisure activities. Moreover, of all leisure activities, watching television is the activity on which the most time is spent (see also United Media, 1982). Both women and men spend more time watching television or listening to the radio than they do on any other type of leisure activity.

Time spent on other leisure activities is not associated with gender, but there are some variations by employment status. Logically, if we were to examine leisure time by gender without controlling for employment, we could expect to observe more gender differences, although they would reflect differences in employment status rather than pure gender effects.

Time spent reading varies by employment status. For both women and men, those who were employed spent significantly less time reading than those who were not employed. Employed men spent three hours less per week reading than men who were not employed. The gap between employed and non-employed women was smaller; employed women spent 3.4 hours per week reading compared to 5.5 hours for women who were not employed. Employment status may affect women's reading less than men's because non-employed women are more likely than men to spend their extra time on household labor (Shamir, 1986). Women who were not employed spent more time participating in social, fraternal and political organizations than those who were employed. Employed women spent less than one hour per week on organizational activities compared to 1.6 hours per week for women who were not employed. Men's time spent in organizations is not significantly associated with their employment status.

As noted previously, time spent watching television is the single leisure activity on which women and men spend the most time. It is also strongly associated with employment status, such that those who are not employed spend significantly more time watching television (and listening to the radio, although this takes up a relatively small portion of the time) than those who are employed. The findings in Table 5.7 regarding the impact of employment status on leisure activities reveal that those who are not employed fill their extra leisure time on passive leisure activities rather than in other, more active, leisure pursuits, and most of the passive leisure time is taken up watching television and listening to the radio.

Leisure activities can also be categorized more generally as active or passive, with passive leisure activities defined as those activities one can do at home as time becomes available. They are less likely to require advance planning or for one to leave the house. Active leisure activities, in contrast, generally require one to leave the house and may require advance planning.

Table 5.8 shows that, when leisure time is classified as active or passive, there is a significant gender gap only in the passive leisure time of those who are not employed; non-employed men spent significantly more time on passive leisure than non-employed women. This pattern is consistent with the pattern for 1975 (Table 5.9). For both years, it is clear that there is a difference in the time use of men and women who are not employed.

Table 5.8
Hours Spent on Passive and Active Leisure Time by Employment Status and Gender, 1981

	Employed		T-test[a]	Not Employed		T-test[b]
	Men	Women		Men	Women	
Passive	19.8	18.8	.96	37.2	30.8	1.94*
	(9.4)	(9.8)		(18.6)	(14.3)	
Active	13.1	12.9	.20	14.5	14.0	.20
	(9.7)	(8.6)		(14.0)	(9.8)	

a. T-test for difference between employed men and women
b. T-test for difference between non-employed men and women
* $p \leq .05$

Table 5.9
Hours Spent on Passive and Active Leisure by Employment
Status and Gender, 1975

	Employed Men	Women	T-test[a]	Not Employed Men	Women	T-test[b]
Passive	19.7 (10.4)	19.1 (9.7)	.71	42.3 (17.8)	28.2 (13.6)	6.05*
Active	10.3 (8.1)	11.1 (8.0)	-1.16	14.3 (13.6)	15.6 (10.0)	-.72

a. T-test for difference between employed men and women
b. T-test for difference between non-employed men and women
* p ≤ .05

Non-employed men have significantly more passive leisure time than non-employed women, although the size of the gap narrowed from 1975 to 1981. Examining Tables 5.7 and 5.8, it is clear that the gap in the passive leisure time between non-employed women and men is a product of men's greater time spent watching television and listening to the radio. Moreover, as argued previously, it may reflect the different characteristics of non-employed women and men; the men are retired while the women are homemakers.

Passive leisure time also varies by a number of other characteristics. As Table 5.10 shows, married men and women generally spend less time on leisure than those who are unmarried. Unmarried men spend slightly more time on both active and passive leisure than unmarried women, and married men spend more time than married women on passive leisure. This may reflect married women's greater time constraints due to their dual responsibilities for household labor and paid labor (Cunningham and Johannis, 1960; Deem, 1982; Shank, 1986).

Table 5.10
Hours Spent on Active and Passive Leisure Time for Employed Men and Women by Marital Status and Number of Children, 1981

| | Active Leisure | | Passive Leisure | |
	Men	Women	Men	Women
Grand Mean	13.1	12.7	19.7	18.9
Marital Status				
Not Married	15.4	12.4	20.7	19.4
Married	12.7	12.9	19.6	18.7
Number of Children				
None	14.6	11.8	20.4	19.7
One	11.1	12.6	20.3	21.4
Two or More	12.5	13.6	19.2	17.0

Active and passive leisure time also vary with number of children, although the pattern is different for active leisure than for passive leisure. Men with children have less active leisure time than those without children, although those with two or more children report more time spent on active leisure than those with only one child. Women's active leisure time is positively associated with number of children. Women's and men's passive leisure time is also associated with number of children such that the more children there are in the household, the less time is spent on passive leisure. The association between number of children and passive leisure time is stronger than the association between number of children and active leisure time. Children may be more likely to affect passive leisure time because passive leisure is accomplished in the household and thus it may be more susceptible to interruption.

Age is associated with time spent on active and passive leisure time, but the association is weak (Table 5.11). In general, older men spend less time on active leisure than younger men, while they spend more time on passive leisure activities. The association is similar for women. In spite of these general patterns, there are significant anomalies in the pattern. For example, men between thirty-five and forty-four spend more time on active leisure than other men, while women aged twenty-five to twenty-nine and forty to forty-four spend the most time on active leisure.

Women's and men's passive and active leisure time vary with education. College-educated men and women spend more time on active leisure than those less well educated, but they spend less time on passive leisure.

Data for 1975 reveal that marital status and number of children were associated with men's and women's active and passive leisure similarly to the pattern observed for 1981. As in 1981, unmarried men spent more time on active leisure pursuits than unmarried women (Table 5.12). Married women and men spent more time on active leisure time in 1981 than in 1975. In 1975, married men spent 9.8 hours per week on active leisure activities compared to 12.7 hours per week in 1981. Thus, the increase in married men's active leisure time from 1975 to 1981 was accompanied by a slight decrease in married men's passive leisure time. Employed married women's active leisure time went from 10.8 hours per week in 1975 to 12.9 hours per week in 1981.

Number of children is associated with women's and men's leisure time in 1975 in a pattern similar to 1981. Men and women with children spent less time on leisure than those without children, although women with children spent more time on active leisure than those with no children.

Table 5.11
Hours Spent on Active and Passive Leisure for Employed Men and Women by Age and Education, 1981

| | Active Leisure | | Passive Leisure | |
	Men	Women	Men	Women
Age				
25-29	11.7	16.4	20.9	19.1
30-34	12.8	12.9	20.8	14.5
35-39	15.1	11.3	18.1	15.6
40-44	15.0	15.4	17.1	17.9
45-49	9.7	9.5	20.4	22.1
50-54	11.2	12.5	20.4	20.3
55+	13.9	11.4	21.3	24.5
Education				
Less Than High School	11.2	10.4	20.2	21.8
High School Degree	11.0	12.7	21.3	19.8
Some College	10.4	12.3	21.3	17.8
College Degree	16.9	14.1	17.5	15.9

Table 5.12
Hours Spent on Active and Passive Leisure for Employed Men and Women by Marital Status and Number of Children, 1975

| | Active Leisure | | Passive Leisure | |
	Men	Women	Men	Women
Grand Mean	10.4	10.9	19.9	19.0
Marital Status				
Not Married	15.9	11.2	19.6	18.2
Married	9.8	10.8	19.9	19.4
Number of Children				
None	11.0	10.1	22.3	21.2
One	9.3	11.3	19.9	19.3
Two or More	10.2	11.6	17.7	16.2

Overall, men spent more time on active leisure in 1981 than in 1975, but the association between age and leisure time was different for the two years (Table 5.13). In 1975, men in their late forties and those in their late twenties spent more time on active leisure than other men. Nevertheless, in most age categories men spent more time on active leisure in 1981 than in 1975. The association between age and passive leisure time was positive for 1975 as it was for 1981, with only a few exceptions. In 1975, the positive association between age and passive leisure time was true except for men in their late forties and men in their late thirties; men in these two age cohorts spent less time on passive leisure than other men. For men in their late forties this low passive leisure time was compensated by high active leisure time, but men in their late thirties had less leisure time than other men. Those age fifty-five or older spent significantly more time on passive leisure than any other age cohort. The high leisure time of those age fifty-five or older probably reflects their lower paid labor time.

For women, the association between age and leisure time is similar in 1975 and 1981, although they generally spent more time on leisure in 1981 than in 1975. With the exception of women in their late thirties, women spent more time on active leisure in 1981 than in 1975. For passive leisure, women under age 45 spent less time in 1981 than in 1975.

Although education was associated with both active and passive leisure time in 1975, the patterns are somewhat different from 1981. Education was curvilinearly associated with active leisure time in 1975. Active leisure time generally declined with increased education for those with less than a college degree. The pattern shifts for those with a college degree. Those with a college degree spent more time on active leisure than those with some college. The association between education and passive leisure time is the same in 1981 and 1975. Those with more education generally spent less time on passive leisure activities than those with less education. This association held for both 1975 and 1981, in spite of the shifts in absolute passive leisure time during the period.

In summary, we see similar patterns of influence on passive and active leisure in 1975 and 1981, although there were shifts in absolute leisure time. The analyses thus far suggest that a number of factors affect leisure time but that gender is not associated with total leisure time, although it is associated with type of leisure activities. I have not, however, evaluated the effects of individual and household characteristics on leisure time while holding constant other variables that may be associated with

Table 5.13
Hours Spent on Active and Passive Leisure for Employed Men and Women by Age and Education, 1975

	Active Leisure Men	Women	Passive Leisure Men	Women
Age				
25-29	11.7	13.1	19.0	19.4
30-34	10.1	10.6	19.4	15.8
35-39	10.1	12.6	17.2	17.4
40-44	10.0	11.4	19.0	19.1
45-49	12.6	8.4	16.3	20.6
50-54	9.4	9.8	21.4	19.1
55+	9.7	10.0	24.6	21.6
Education				
Less Than High School	10.2	10.1	22.2	20.0
High School Degree	11.3	11.4	19.5	19.1
Some College	8.8	9.6	21.1	18.6
College Degree	10.2	11.4	18.3	17.8

leisure. Moreover, we may find that paid labor and household labor affect women's and men's leisure time differently.

MULTIVARIATE ANALYSES OF LEISURE TIME

As was the case with paid labor time and household labor time, multivariate analyses of the determinants of leisure will allow identification of those variables associated with leisure time, with the confounding effects of other variables removed. Gender is included in the multivariate analyses to determine if, after other characteristics are held constant, women's and men's leisure time varies. Employment status and paid labor time are included so that the independent effects of participation in the paid labor force and hours spent in paid labor on leisure time can be estimated. I expect that being employed has an effect on leisure that is distinct from the impact of actual hours spent in paid labor.

Other research as well as the bivariate analyses presented earlier in Chapter 5 indicate that household labor is associated with leisure time; thus household labor time is included as an independent variable in the equations. Exploratory analyses revealed no significant interactions between paid labor time and gender or household labor time and gender; thus the interaction terms were excluded from the analyses.

Marital status is associated with leisure time in bivariate analyses and the association is somewhat different for women and men; thus I have included marital status and a marital status/gender interaction term in the equations. Age also may be associated with leisure time to the extent to which it is associated with life-course events. Because the association may be curvilinear I have included age and age-squared. Given differences in the timing of life course events, the gender and age interaction terms allow identification of gender differences in the association between age and leisure time.

Finally, education may be associated with leisure. Earlier bivariate analyses revealed that education was associated with type of leisure, as well as with total leisure time, but that there was no gender difference in the association. Thus, I have included education as an independent variable in the MRAs.

MRA is used to evaluate the determinants of total leisure time as well as active leisure time and passive leisure time separately. Earlier analyses suggest that some of the independent variables may be associated more strongly with type of leisure than with total leisure time.

The multivariate analysis of total leisure time presented in Table 5.14 shows that paid labor time, household labor time and marital status are associated with leisure time after other characteristics have been taken into account. The more time respondents spent in paid labor, the less time they spent on leisure activities. For each additional hour men and women spent in paid labor they spend .61 of an hour less on leisure. Similarly, for each additional hour men and women spend on household labor they spend .64 of an hour less on leisure. Although some researchers have suggested that the effects of paid labor time and household labor time on leisure time vary by gender (Clark et al., 1978; Shaw, 1985), my findings reveal no gender differences in the effects.

Marital status is significantly associated with total leisure time similarly for women and men. Married respondents spent 3.5 fewer hours on leisure per week than those who were not married. Thus, the bivariate association between marital status and leisure time observed earlier is not merely a function of housework and paid labor time, but reflects an independent effect of marital status on leisure time.

At least with respect to total leisure time it is clear that both paid labor time and household labor time are strongly associated with leisure time. The lack of gender differences in the effects does not mean that, in fact, household labor time is not the greater impediment to women's leisure time, nor that paid labor time is not the bigger impediment to men. To the extent to which women's household labor time is greater than men's and men's paid labor time higher than women's, there will be differences in the constraints on their leisure time.

Table 5.14
Total, Active and Passive Leisure by Gender, Employment Status, Paid Labor Time, Household Labor Time, Marital Status, Marital*Gender, Age, Age*Gender, Age², Age²*Gender and Education for All Women and Men, 1981

	Total Leisure	Active Leisure	Passive Leisure
Gender	-15.7	11.0	-27.7*
	(10.5)	(9.2)	(11.1)
Employment Status	-1.0	3.3*	-4.1*
	(1.6)	(1.4)	(1.7)
Paid Labor Time	-.61***	-.31***	-.28***
	(.03)	(.03)	(.04)
Household Labor Time	-.64***	-.30***	-.32***
	(.04)	(.04)	(.05)
Marital Status	-3.5+	-1.5	-1.0
	(1.8)	(1.6)	(1.9)
Marital*Gender	2.2	-.04	1.3
	(2.3)	(2.0)	(2.4)
Age	-.02	-.46	-.50^ᵃ
	(.35)	(.31)	(.37)
Age*Gender	.50	-.49	1.05*
	(.43)	(.38)	(.46)
Age²	-.001	-.01*	.005-
	(.003)	(.003)	(.004)
Age²*Gender	-.005	-.005	-.01*
	(.004)	(.004)	(.004)
Education	-.19	.38**	-.48**
	(.16)	(.14)	(.16)
Constant	78.1	15.4	59.7
	(8.7)	(7.6)	(9.2)
R²	.56	.19	.34
Number	491	491	491

a. Significance levels for women.
Significance levels for men: *** p ≤ .001, ** p ≤ .01, * p ≤ .05, + p ≤ .1
Significance levels for women:^^^ p ≤ .001, ^^ p ≤ .01, ^ p ≤ .05, - p ≤ .1

Overall, this model explains 56% of the variation in leisure time. I can, therefore, conclude that time spent on leisure is largely determined by time spent in paid work and household labor. To the extent to which employed women spend more time working than men (including both paid labor and unpaid household labor), some of the costs of this double day come in the form of reduced leisure time (Meissner et al., 1975; Shaw, 1985).

Given that men's and women's time spent on passive and active leisure is different, that age is associated with type of leisure activities, and that passive and active leisure activities may be subject to different kinds of constraints, we may be able to more fully understand leisure time expenditures if we examine the determinants of active and passive leisure time separately.

Determinants of Active and Passive Leisure Time

In my equations examining active and passive leisure time separately, some effects are different from the determinants of total leisure time. Active leisure time is associated with paid labor time, household labor time, education, age and a variable indicating whether the respondent was employed or not. The employment indicator and paid labor time variables allow us to determine the independent effects of simply being employed as well as of hours spent in paid labor on active leisure time.

Gender is not associated with active leisure time, nor are there any significant interaction effects indicating that any of the independent variables affect active leisure time differently for men than for women. Employment status and paid labor time are associated with active leisure time. Those who are employed spend 3.3 more hours on active leisure than those who are not employed. Time spent in paid labor is, however, negatively associated with active leisure time. For each additional hour spent in paid labor, respondents spent .31 of an hour less time (18.6 minutes) on active leisure. Thus, being employed is positively associated with active leisure time, but, once employed, time spent in paid labor is negatively associated with active leisure time.

The positive effect of being employed on active leisure time also indicates that those who are not employed spend less time on active leisure than the employed. In addition, the more time one spends on household labor the less time is spent on active leisure. For each additional hour spent on household labor, respondents spent .30 of an hour less (eighteen minutes) on active leisure. Thus, household labor time and paid labor time affect active leisure in similar ways. In addition, there are no gender differences in the effects of paid labor time and household labor time on active leisure time.

Education is positively associated with active leisure time even after other variables have been taken into account. For each additional year of education, respondents spent .38 of an hour more time on active leisure. This 22.8 minute increase for each year of education confirms my earlier finding regarding the association between education and active leisure time.

The association between age and active leisure time is less clear. Although age-squared is negatively associated with active leisure time, the positive association between age and active leisure time is not statistically significant. Given the small sample size and the high correlation between age and age-squared, it is more difficult for coefficients to reach statistical significance. Nevertheless, the coefficient for age is nearly significant at $p < .13$. We can be fairly confident, therefore, that the association between age and active leisure time is curvilinear (this is supported by plotting age against active leisure time). Active leisure time appears to be positively associated with age up to age thirty-eight and negatively associated with it after age thirty-eight.

My model accounts for 19% of the variation in active leisure time. We can conclude from this that a number of other factors, not included in my model, are associated with active leisure time. Some of the factors may be those associated with type of leisure activities rather than with time spent on leisure activities.

The determinants of passive leisure time are somewhat different from the determinants of active leisure time. In addition to employment status, paid labor time, household labor time, education and age, gender also affects passive leisure time. In addition, some of the effects are different from those for active leisure time.

Employment status is associated with passive leisure time, but the direction of the association is different than for active leisure time. Those who are employed spent 4.1 fewer hours per week on passive leisure time than those who are not employed. This finding, combined with the finding that employed respondents spend more time on active leisure time, tells us that employed respondents spend their leisure time differently than those who are not employed. That is, those who are employed are more likely to spend their leisure time on active leisure activities than is the case for those who are not employed.

Time spent in paid labor is also negatively associated with passive leisure time. For each additional hour respondents spent in paid labor they spent .28 of an hour (16.8 minutes) less on passive leisure. Being employed negatively affects passive leisure time and the more time the employed spent in paid labor, the less time they spent on passive leisure.

Household labor time is also negatively associated with passive leisure time. For every hour spent on household labor, respondents spent .32 of an hour less time on passive leisure. This effect is similar to the effect on active leisure time. Thus, although passive leisure may be more "interruptable" by household tasks, it does not appear to be affected any more than active leisure time.

Education is negatively associated with passive leisure time. For each additional year of education respondents spent almost half an hour less on passive leisure. This effect is opposite the effect of education on active leisure time, indicating that education is associated with type of leisure activities more than with amount of leisure time.

Age is the one variable whose association with passive leisure time varies by gender. For men, age is not significantly associated with passive leisure time once other variables have been taken into account. The significant interaction terms for the age variables indicate that there is a gender difference in the impact of age on passive leisure time. By adding the coefficients for the interaction terms to the coefficients for the age variables, we can see that age is positively associated with women's passive leisure time. The negative sign on the age-squared variable indicates that this positive association persists only for respondents who are under age fifty-seven. After that point age is negatively associated with passive leisure time.

Although gender is not associated with either total leisure time or active leisure time, it is associated with passive leisure time. Holding other variables constant, women spent significantly less time on passive leisure than men. Table 5.10 reveals that even without taking other characteristics into account, men spent more time on passive leisure than women. The effect is, however, much larger once other variables, notably paid labor time and household labor time, are taken into account. Thus, although gender does not appear to be significantly associated with total leisure time, it is associated with type of leisure. Even though the effect of gender on active leisure time is not significant at $p < .05$, the association is positive, which would indicate that women have more active leisure time than men. With a larger sample, the gender effect might have been significant for active leisure time as well as for passive leisure time.

My equation explains 34% of the variation in passive leisure time. We are clearly able to account for more of the variation in passive leisure time than in active leisure time, perhaps indicating that passive leisure is more affected by time constraints than is active leisure time. We have seen that paid labor time and household labor time affect leisure time and that the size of the effect is similar for women and men. In spite of similarities in the size of the effects, total leisure time may vary with total work time (both paid and unpaid household) and there may be gender differences in the pattern. In Table 5.15 I examine men's and women's total leisure time by total work time.

Among those whose total time spent on housework and paid work is from zero to thirty hours per week, men spent 56.7 hours

Table 5.15
Total Leisure by Total Work Time and Gender for All Women and Men, 1981

Total Work Time	Men	Women
0-30	56.7	49.0
31-40	44.2	29.9
41-55	37.2	34.1
56+	27.2	24.6

per week on leisure, compared to forty-nine hours for women. For both women and men, total work time is negatively associated with total leisure time, but within every category men spent more time on leisure than women. What do women do with their time if they do not use it for leisure? Although they may spend some of their available time sleeping, it is more likely that the time is spent on childcare. My measures of time use include paid labor, leisure and housework, but I have not included childcare in the housework measure largely because a good measure of childcare is not available for all years. These findings indirectly indicate that, in addition to paid labor and household labor, women probably spend more time than men on childcare, as evidenced by their reduced leisure time.

CONCLUSION

Although there are significant differences between women's and men's paid labor time and household labor time, their leisure *time* is not very different. Men and women have similar amounts of leisure time, and the pattern of change in leisure time from 1975 to 1981 was the same. In spite of the similarities in their leisure time, men's and women's specific leisure activities vary. Men watch more television and spend more time on sports than women, while women spend more time socializing than men. In addition, especially among women who are not employed, some leisure time is very closely related to household labor. Non-employed women spend over four hours per week on hobbies, and the single most time consuming hobby is preserving and canning fruits and vegetables.

Both household labor time and paid labor time affect leisure, but there are no gender differences in their impact on leisure time (see also Nock and Kingston, 1989). Thus, each additional hour spent on either paid labor or household labor affects men's and women's leisure time in the same way. Analyses in Chapters 3 and 4 showed that men continue to spend more time in paid labor than women and women spend more time on household labor than men. Thus, paid labor will be more likely to affect men's leisure simply because they spend more time in paid labor. Similarly, women's relatively high household labor time makes it more likely that household labor time will affect their leisure time than is the case for men.

Chapter 5 also showed that, after time expenditures and other personal characteristics have been taken into account, the only remaining gender effect is its effect on passive leisure time. Women spent significantly less time on passive leisure than men, most likely reflecting men's greater time spent watching television.

The gender influenced pattern of time use observed in men's and women's paid labor and household labor time has little impact on women's and men's overall leisure time, although we do see some differences in their specific leisure activities. These differences may, however, result from differences in preferences as much as from differences in time constraints. In the final chapter,

I assess the significance of the findings thus far and evaluate their implications for changing gender roles.

NOTES

1. John Robinson also argues that the perception that the United States is, in general, short of time may reflect the large number of people in their thirties and forties. He asserts that people in their thirties and forties have less discretionary time (Hall, 1991). This argument is consistent with the findings reported here.

2. Although Robinson has argued that leisure time is actually increasing, my analyses of leisure time expenditures in 1975 and 1981 reveal few changes in men's or women's leisure time from 1975 to 1981 (Hall, 1991).

6

Conclusion

The analyses presented in this book show that paid work and household responsibilities not only impact on each other but may conflict. That is, time spent in one sphere means less time spent in another. If commitments to paid labor and household labor call for full-time participation in both, that time must come either at the expense of leisure or else some of the demands of paid labor and household labor must go unmet.

The situation of CBS's Meredith Viera is a visible example of how paid work and household responsibilities may conflict and require some sort of sacrifice. CBS did not allow Viera to work part-time on "60 Minutes" in order to accommodate her work to the demands of her family; thus her career was sacrificed, at least in the short term, to her household responsibilities.

The data on paid labor and household labor also illustrate that although there has been some change in men's and women's time use patterns, significant gender differences persist. Moreover, just as one has to understand Meredith Viera's paid work demands to understand her time spent on household labor, one also must understand her paid labor time in terms of her household responsibilities. My findings indicate that Viera's situation is not unique. When looking at nationally representative samples we find that family responsibilities affect paid labor time. Thus, while it may be possible to coordinate paid labor and household responsibilities, as Viera was able to do until recently, the demands of the paid labor force and the household often conflict. The coordination of paid labor and household demands often takes the form of reduced hours in paid labor and reduced time spent on household labor. Thus, women may work part-time and use substitutes for some of their household labor. Necessitated by the dual demands of paid labor and household labor, this compromise that women often manage is different from men's coordination of household and paid labor responsibilities. Not only do men spend significantly less time on household labor than women, but this pattern reflects the differences between women's and men's household responsibilities. Women often face Viera's dilemma, while men generally do not confront such a set of choices (Miller and Garrison, 1982). Even with recent changes in the normative expectations of fathers, men's breadwinner role typically remains dominant.

CHANGE IN PAID LABOR, HOUSEHOLD LABOR AND LEISURE TIME: A REPRISE

There were significant changes in men's and women's time use from 1975 to 1987. The different patterns of change have resulted in some convergence in time use patterns, although significant differences remain. From 1975 to 1987, not only did women's rates of labor force participation increase while men's decreased, but the amount of time that employed women spent in paid labor increased as well. During this same period, employed men reduced the actual number of hours they spent in paid labor. These divergent trends resulted in an increase in the ratio of women's paid labor time to men's paid labor time. Employed women spent over 80% as much time as men in paid labor in 1987, compared to just over 71% in 1975. In spite of convergence, however, a significant gap in the paid labor time of women and men remains.

During the same period in which women increased their paid labor time, popular descriptions characterized men as increasing their household labor time. In fact, from 1975 to 1987 employed men's housework as a percentage of women's increased from 46% to 57.5%. Thus, women's and men's paid labor time became more similar than did their housework time. In addition, a significant part of the convergence in women's and men's housework time was a function of a decrease in women's housework time rather than an increase in men's housework time.

The convergence in women's and men's household labor time was also greater among those who are younger than among those who are older. In spite of the convergence in housework time, not only does a significant time gap remain but significant differences in men's and women's housework tasks remain as well. Women continue to be primarily responsible for indoor household tasks while men spend more time on outdoor tasks. In addition, the most strongly gender-typed tasks remain that way; women continue to spend significantly more time than men preparing meals, completing indoor cleaning and doing laundry.

Finally, in examining the patterns of change in women's and men's leisure time we find that there is little difference in women's and men's total leisure time and that the nature of change from 1975 to 1981 was similar for women and men. Overall, both women and men spent slightly less time on leisure in 1981 than they did in 1975, although the shifts in types of leisure activities were greater. Time spent on passive leisure time declined from 1975 to 1981. Some of the decline in passive leisure time was replaced by active leisure time. Nevertheless, both women and men spent more time in passive leisure than in active leisure in 1975 and 1981.

There were differences in women's and men's leisure activities and these were relatively stable from 1975 to 1981. That is, although men's and women's passive leisure time declined from 1975 to 1981, men continued to spend more time on passive leisure than women. Examination of specific leisure activities reveals that most of men's additional passive leisure time is spent watching television or listening to the radio.

I have documented changes in women's and men's time use patterns, but the changes were not as great as one might expect. Men's and women's paid labor time and household labor time became more similar, but significant differences remain. Moreover, leisure time expenditures changed slightly, but the changes were similar for women and men. For both women and men, however, 1981 was not characterized by significantly more leisure time than 1975, in spite of the descriptions of some (Hall, 1991; Parker, 1976).

Determinants of Time Use

Although there were changes in men's and women's time use patterns from 1975 to 1987, differences persist, as do differences in the influences on women's and men's time use. Married men and men with children devote more time to paid labor than do men without such responsibilities, while married women and women with children spend less time on paid labor than do women who are not married or do not have children. The findings with respect to the influence of family status on paid labor time indicate that the demands of the household on men are at least partly financial (Bernard, 1981). Thus, in order to fulfill their household and paid labor demands, men do not have to coordinate and compromise because the demands of the household are consistent with the demands of the labor market. For women, however, the relationship between family status and paid labor time indicates that women with family obligations are less able to spend time in paid labor than women without such obligations. Thus, although the paid labor time of women with spouses and children has been increasing in recent years, these women continue to spend less time in paid labor than do women without spouses or children.

Of course, not all of the household demands on men are financial. Men as well as women spend time on housework, but the key difference is that men spend less time on housework than do women. By spending less time, men are better able to complete their household tasks without altering their paid labor time. Employed men's twenty-one hours of housework per week can more easily be accomplished on the weekend and in the evening, not only because it is twenty-one hours, compared to thirty-five hours for employed women, but because their household tasks are different than women's. More of men's housework time is spent on outdoor tasks than on meal preparation. Outdoor tasks, while certainly necessary, are more discretionary, at least with respect to scheduling. The lawn can go unmowed for an extra day or week. Women's household tasks, on the other hand, are less discretionary. If work runs long, a meal cannot be put off until tomorrow. As such, women's household responsibilities are more likely to have an impact on their paid labor, require conscious coordination with paid labor time, and necessitate replacement if paid labor demands are high.

Further evidence of the dual demands often placed on women can be seen by comparing the amount of time spent on both paid work and housework by those who are employed at least forty hours per week. The total work time of men employed forty hours per week is seventy hours, while women employed forty hours per week spend seventy-seven hours per week working. Thus, among those employed full-time women spend approximately seven more hours per week than do men on housework and paid work combined. This figure is a conservative estimate of the difference because it does not include childcare time. Data on the average childcare time of women and men indicate that among those whose total work time is fifty-five hours per week or more, women spend over an hour more per week on childcare. This finding is consistent with research by Steven Nock and Paul William Kingston (1988) that shows that even in dual-earner households, women spend significantly more time on childcare than do men. Moreover, no matter what the total work time (paid labor and household labor combined), women spend more time on childcare than men. As we saw in Chapter 5, even after controlling for total work time, women spend less time on leisure than men. This pattern, once again, probably reflects women's greater childcare time.

In addition to affecting the amount of leisure time available to women and men, paid labor and household labor may account for some of women's and men's leisure activities. Women's greater time spent on leisure activities like preserving fruits and vegetables could be categorized as time spent on housework, albeit somewhat more discretionary housework. Men's greater time spent watching television may reflect patterns of time use related to housework and childcare. It is a truism to point out that the image of the household in the evening includes a man watching television and a woman cooking dinner or washing the dishes. Thus, the gender gap in television hours may indicate that women have less time *at home* when they can sit and watch television because their household responsibilities are more likely to intrude than is the case for men.

EXPLANATIONS FOR TIME USE PATTERNS

In addition to highlighting the interrelationships among household labor, paid labor and leisure, the analyses presented here have assessed the explanatory power of a number of proposed explanations for women's and men's time spent on household labor, as well as for the gap in their household labor time. My findings reveal that the observed gender gap in household labor time is the product of differences between women and men as well as differences in the impact of some characteristics on household labor time, rather than a direct effect of gender. For example, family status affects men and women differently because the *demands* of a family are different for women than for men. In addition, as expected, I found that paid labor time affects women's household labor time more than men's. This reflects differences in women's and men's household tasks, with women more often performing tasks that cannot be coordinated with paid labor demands. Of course, household demands also impact on paid labor time, as noted in Chapter 3. In addition to time constraints or paid labor demands associated with less household labor time, there are demands associated with more household labor time. Children represent a demand on men and women to spend more time on household labor. Men and women with children spend more time on household labor than those without children, although the presence of children affects women's household labor time more than men's.

Time constraints are therefore important influences on women's and men's time use, although the same characteristics may represent different sorts of demands for women and men. In addition, we know that the costs associated with time spent on household labor are correlated with actual time expenditures. Thus, education is negatively associated with women's household labor time, just as occupational status is negatively associated with women's and men's household labor time.

Most of the theorizing about household labor has focused on the size of the gap between women's and men's household labor time and, thus, on household labor time within married (or cohabiting) couple households. There has been considerable attention given to the impact on household labor time of the interaction between women's and men's characteristics. That is, respondents' household labor time is seen to be affected by respondents', spouses'/partners' and households' characteristics. In this study I established that spouses'/partners' characteristics may affect respondents' household labor time. Among a subsample of married and unmarried cohabiting respondents, I found that while time constraints affect household labor time, those time constraints may come in the form of demands on spouses' time. I also found that, while the relative resources of respondents and their spouses/partners were not significantly associated with either men's or women's household labor time, attitudes were associated with household labor time. Moreover, the costs of participating in household labor, as measured by education, continue to be associated with household labor time even after other resources have been taken into account.

Spouses' paid labor time is positively associated with respondents' household labor time and represents a constraint on spouses' ability to spend time on household labor. The more time a respondent's spouse spends in paid labor, the more time the respondent spends on household labor. Although I expected spouses' household labor time to be negatively associated with respondents' household labor time (since it could be a substitute), I found that the more time a spouse spent on household labor, the more time a respondent spent.

Nevertheless, my results reinforce my earlier interpretation that time constraints represent a significant influence on time use. From the analyses of paid labor time presented here, however, *we know that time constraints are gender specific*. Thus, having children or a spouse has a different effect on time use for women and men. In some sense, it is our gender-specific conceptions of appropriate behavior that lead to the differences in paid labor time and household labor time. Moreover, attitudes about how work should be distributed have an independent effect on household labor time. Men with egalitarian sex role attitudes and women with traditional sex role attitudes spend more time on household labor than men with traditional sex role attitudes or women with egalitarian attitudes.

My analyses also show that time constraints in the form of paid labor and household labor are the only factors affecting total leisure time, although education, age and gender are associated with the type of leisure activities on which respondents spend their time. These findings illustrate some of the costs associated with women's double day, as well as the benefits of not having a double day. The extra time that employed women spend on household labor comes at least partly at the expense of their leisure. Thus, women with dual responsibilities not only have a greater number and variety of responsibilities, but these responsibilities affect their leisure time.

My findings on leisure also indicate that more of women's leisure time may be, in fact, household labor, while men's leisure time is more likely to be unrelated to household labor. Of course, it is possible that some of the time men spend on sports activities is related to their employment. That is, men may be more likely to play golf or basketball with co-workers. As such, some of the differences between men's and women's leisure time investments may reflect their differential involvement in paid labor and household labor, respectively.

PROMOTING EQUALITY

In addition to identifying the complex interrelationships among paid labor, household labor and leisure, the analyses presented in this book illustrate the problems inherent in efforts to understand or change women's labor force participation, including their occupational segregation, without also focusing on women's continued responsibility for household labor. Without a reduction in women's household labor time, full participation in the paid labor force is impossible. Not only do women employed full-time continue to spend over thirty-five hours per week on housework, they are primarily responsible for non-discretionary household tasks. These household responsibilities necessarily conflict with women's participation in the paid labor force because they are not always tasks that can be scheduled around work demands.

The gender gap in paid labor time will remain unless household labor is redistributed and the paid labor demands on women and men altered. Simply allowing women to schedule work to accommodate household demands is likely to be insufficient because it retains the difference between women and men. After allowing Viera to work part-time for two years, Don Hewitt at CBS said that he needs a full-time person who will handle the same number of stories as Mike Wallace or Ed Bradley. The problem is, then, that work—and not only Viera's high-profile work—is not structured so as to accommodate family and household responsibilities. The assumption implicit in the design of a "60 Minutes" job and many other jobs is that holders of those jobs can devote a set number of hours to the job and that there will be little or no conflict with household demands. The presumed lack of conflict with household demands reflects the assumption that job holders have no significant time-intensive household demands. As I argued previously, household demands are expected to require labor force participation, not inhibit it.

It is questionable that women want to increase their paid labor time, but as Myra Marx Ferree (1987) has argued, women's lack of expressed desire to spend more time in paid labor may reflect their poor work conditions as much as it reflects their desire to spend time on household labor. Moreover, women's labor force participation, like men's, is largely the result of economic need. Thus, the issue of promoting greater equality in ability to participate in the paid labor force is an economic issue. That is, whether women wish to spend time in paid labor or not, economic circumstances often require that they do, and to the extent that women remain responsible for household labor and employers do not recognize workers' household responsibilities, equality of opportunity is denied.

Employers are unlikely to structure work in order to allow both women and men to fulfill household responsibilities without some pressure to do so. Issues raised by women have produced some changes in business' responses to women's demands for schedules that allow them to fulfill household responsibilities. Companies are more likely to allow flexible scheduling and part-time work than they were in the past, but there are limits to the flexibility—as we saw with Viera—and, for the most part, men have not been either able or willing to use flexible scheduling or part-time work to allow them to spend more time on household labor. Men's failure to change their work patterns means that the definition of full participation in the paid labor force remains unchanged. That is, the absence of household responsibilities impinging on work time remains the expectation and the standard against which workers are measured.

Even those who argue that women are an indispensable part of the labor force often discuss the "costs" of employing women that arise from their household responsibilities (Schwartz, 1989).

These costs are compared to the lack of any such "household-induced" costs for men; the *ideal* worker is still seen as one without household responsibilities. Schwartz goes so far as to advocate a "career" or "family" track for women (but not for men) in order to allow women to self-select into the family or career track as distinct from the normative "male" career track.

If all workers came to expect work to be structured so that they could coordinate household and paid labor responsibilities, the "costs" of employing women would not be seen as unusual, any more than health care expenditures are seen as unusual costs. That is, full-time work is currently most often structured without thought to childcare or housework demands. For example, employers may expect workers to stay after hours with little or no notice, not expecting them to have household responsibilities that would prohibit their participation in late meetings (e.g., meal preparation). If household labor were shared more equally between women and men, late meetings without notice would not be seen as a problem for *women*, per se, but as inappropriate for all workers, just as work without health benefits is seen as unacceptable for many workers now. Thus, rather than proposing strategies that allow women to coordinate household and paid labor responsibilities, energy might more fruitfully be expended on efforts to redistribute household responsibilities and change work expectations for both women and men. It is clear that work and family are related for both men and women. Yet men's relative freedom from household labor gives them more access to employment, while women's household labor responsibilities limit their paid labor opportunities.

Although there are few examples of flexible scheduling and other employer policies that allow employees to coordinate family and work responsibilities, there are enough examples and sufficient research to begin to assess the impact of employer policies on women's and men's time use patterns. Not surprisingly, some researchers see the changes that have occurred as indicating that change is forthcoming, while others view changes in employers' policies as examples of how little is being done.

Family-Responsive Policies

Family-responsive policies take a variety of forms and range from fairly comprehensive programs to small informational services. The strategies adopted by some employers include flexible scheduling, job–sharing, parental leave, childcare information, and child care services. Along with the diversity in the types of policies adopted, we might expect differences in the extent to which the policies address the work/family conflicts faced by employees.

Flexible scheduling takes a variety of forms. Employees may be allowed to vary their schedules daily, weekly or on some other basis so that they can schedule their work to minimize the conflict with household obligations. For example, an employee may work from 10:00 A.M. until 6:00 P.M., rather than from 9:00 A.M. until 5:00 P.M. Workers may be able to work more hours one week and fewer hours another, although this may create problems of overtime compensation for some employees (Christensen and Staines, 1990). Other companies may simply have a band of hours during which employees must be at work, but additional hours may be worked at the employees' convenience (Christensen and Staines, 1990).

Job-sharing and permanent part-time work also are flexible scheduling options that may be adopted. Job-sharing occurs when two employees share one full-time position. The benefit of job-sharing is that it allows employees to work fewer hours, yet they retain the benefits and responsibilities of a full-time position (Kingston, 1990). That is, the part-time position held by each member of the job-sharing team typically is different from most part-time positions. Permanent part-time positions are another option. Part-time positions generally offer fewer rewards than full-time positions as well as less job security (Kingston, 1990). Job-sharing, though rare, is a way that these disadvantages of part-time employment can be partly alleviated (Pleck, 1989). Even with responsibility and benefits commensurate with full-time work, job-sharing and part-time employment may not be viable options for coordinating work and family demands. These jobs pay, at best, significantly less than full-time positions simply because of the reduced number of hours.

Parental leave policies are not permanent solutions to the conflicts between work and household demands, but they are short-term solutions to time demands created by the birth or illness of a child or the care requirements of a parent. An example of a comprehensive parental leave policy that addresses gender equity issues is the policy of Sweden. As Linda Haas (1990) reports, Sweden allows parents to take up to one year off work for the care of a newborn child at close to full pay. Additional time off at reduced pay also may be arranged. The policy is explicitly designed to encourage a change in men's and women's roles in the household. The dual roles of both mothers and fathers are addressed in the Swedish policy. By allowing and even encouraging fathers to take time off to care for a child, the government hopes to change men's involvement in child care and household tasks. Although 27% of Swedish fathers take advantage of the paid parental leave, more women take advantage of it. Moreover, after returning to work, Swedish women are more likely to prefer part-time employment than are men, even though men who take parental leave spend fewer hours in paid employment, earn less and may spend more time with their young children than men who do not take leave (Haas, 1990; Lamb et al., 1988).

As Pleck (1989) has argued, until quite recently parental leave in the United States has been defined as "maternity leave" and has been available only to women. It is further defined as a temporary leave for medical reasons related to childbirth. Thus, few employers offer even maternity leave to adopting parents. The time off is most often viewed as necessary in order for the mother to recuperate from childbirth. When parental leave is an option it may take a variety of forms, including paid leave and unpaid leave, short-term leave, use of sick leave, or leave arranged informally. As Kingston (1990) points out, it is often difficult to assess the real operation of leave policies since employers may have formal policies that are not followed.

Even when parental leave is available to both women and men, women are more likely to take it than men (Pleck, 1989; Trost, 1988). The hesitance of fathers to take parental leave may reflect a number of perceived barriers. In addition to the variety of forms that parental leave can take, those who take it may also be treated in a variety of ways. Rather than interpreting fathers' general reluctance to take leave as indicative of their lack of desire to do so, we might also focus on the perceived *costs* of parental leave. Thus, a company may offer parental leave, and even have a formal policy stipulating that employees who take leave will not be "punished," but the reality may be different. Just as women may suffer career setbacks as a result of taking advantage of parental leave, men may suffer even greater career fallout (Pleck, 1989). Although many companies require complete career dedication, often measured by a willingness to work long hours, refuse vacations and accept transfers, they are still more likely to accept the intrusion of family responsibilities for women than for men. Men who take leave may be more likely to be seen as "choosing" family over career, while for women family obligations may be less likely to be seen as a choice.

Of course, not all men have jobs where they are expected to be "committed." For these men, as well as for men with jobs requiring greater time commitments, taking time off work for family obligations may be seen as suspect by friends, family and neighbors. Men who stay home to care for a child are far more likely to be called upon to *explain* their behavior than are women. For although women's roles in the labor market and in the household have changed, women are still more likely to be seen as *responsible* for the care of children. As such, a woman's decision to spend time out of the labor force is more readily accepted as *normal*, in fact it may be expected, than is a man's decision to do the same (Lamb, 1987).

In spite of the infrequency with which men take parental leave, the *Wall Street Journal* (1988) reports that the number of men taking parental leave has been increasing. Nevertheless, since there are a variety of ways in which men may take parental leave, and it is clear that they are not doing so to any great extent, we may be unwise to expect that changes in the division of household labor and responsibility will be induced by the provision of parental leave.

Employer-provided childcare information and services also are ways in which employers may attempt to help employees accommodate work and family demands. A number of employers offer childcare information and referral services (Galinsky and Stein, 1990) while others offer on-site or subsidized childcare services. Auerbach (1990:398) suggests that employer-sponsored childcare services may foster change because they represent the "institutional expression of the acceptance of mothers working and the acceptance of extrafamilial childcare." Nevertheless, employer sponsored childcare is still rare and it is more likely to be available in larger worksites. Employees at small worksites, those less likely to provide childcare services, earn less than those who work in large worksites. As a result, the workers most in need of childcare services are those who are least likely to receive them. This is much like flexible scheduling; flexible scheduling is more likely to be available to well-paid employees and these employees are the ones least likely to need it. Nevertheless, employer-sponsored childcare services are gender neutral and do not require either men or women to sacrifice their careers or earnings to take advantage of them. In addition, extrafamilial childcare reduces the workload in the household by reducing childcare time as well as by reducing housework time. Housework time is reduced simply because the house is inhabited fewer hours per day. If, as Janet Hunt and Larry Hunt (1987) argue, men are not likely to pick up additional household labor, women may be able to accommodate household and work demands by reducing one or the other of them. It is often too expensive to reduce paid work demands; and to do so also reinforces women's subordinate role in the labor market and thereby reinforces their responsibility for household labor.

As I have shown, time constraints are associated with household labor time. Thus, if women take advantage of any kind of
reduced work schedule they have more time for household labor.
Employer-sponsored flexible schedules may, therefore, allow
women to accommodate work and household demands, but in so
doing they may reinforce the gender gap in household labor time
as well as in responsibility for the emotional and financial needs
of the household. Unless both men and women are willing and
able to take advantage of flexible scheduling, parental leave or
other family-responsive policies, the current trend toward offering some assistance in accommodating work and family demands
may as well be called mother- or woman-responsive policies.

The symmetrical family (Young and Willmott, 1973) is not now
the norm. Women have increased their responsibility for paid
labor but large changes in men's responsibility for household
tasks, or even in their time spent on household tasks, have not
accompanied this change. In addition, although men are more
likely to take advantage of employer-sponsored leave for the care
of children than in the past, women are still far more likely to
interrupt their careers or jobs to care for children. In addition,
because of women's greater time spent on housework in general,
household demands are more likely to impact on women's labor
force participation than is the case for men.

Thus, although the segregation of women's and men's roles in
the labor market and in the household has decreased, women's
roles have changed more than men's, resulting in only limited
change overall. Employer-sponsored policies to ease the conflicts
between work and family are more likely to be used by women
and therefore to reinforce women's responsibility for the household. Further change in men's household roles might be fostered
by employer policies that allow women and men greater flexibility
in scheduling their work day without identifying that flexibility
as a means to accommodate family demands. In addition, acute
conflicts between work and family could be accommodated by
offering occasional sabbaticals to employees. By having sabbaticals rather than parental leave, men, as well as women, might be

encouraged to take advantage of the time off without fear of loss of promotion opportunities (Pleck, 1990). This also would remedy the inequity introduced when only those with particular family responsibilities are allowed to have leaves.

As research on family-responsive policies shows and as the pace of change in women's and men's patterns of time use indicates, change is likely to be slow in coming. For the near future, women's labor force opportunities will continue to be constrained by their family responsibilities while men's employment opportunities are enhanced by their relative lack of conflicting family responsibilities. Moreover, we can expect the current patterns of leisure activities to continue, with men having access to more passive leisure (e.g., television) while women continue to spend more time on productive leisure activities (e.g., canning fruits and vegetables).

Although the era of the two-person career is over, jobs generally have not been redesigned to reflect this new reality. Few women or men can devote time to their paid jobs as if they have no other demands on their time. Men are no longer likely to be married to full-time homemakers who relieve them of household responsibilities. Women never had wives to maintain the household, but they have either entered jobs designed for women with household demands and suffered the low wages, or they have entered jobs where no accommodation to household demands is allowed. The change in women's roles has, therefore, created conflict between work and family for both women and men, even if the conflicts still are felt more by women than by men. The strains are there for men as well, especially younger men who are most likely to have spouses/partners who participate in the paid labor force. Thus, it is insufficient simply to renegotiate work and family responsibilities between women and men. Work demands also must be altered to reflect the reality of family demands on both women and men.

Appendix: Categories of Time Use

1975-1981 STUDY OF TIME USE

Household Tasks

meal preparation: cooking, fixing lunches
meal preparation: serving, setting table
washing dishes
meal cleanup, clearing table
miscellaneous work around the house
routine indoor cleaning/housework
routine outdoor cleaning: yardwork, snow removal, cutting lawn
laundry: wash clothes
laundry: iron, mend, fold, put away clothes
indoor repairs and maintenance: painting, plumbing
car care: tune-up, routine care
home improvements: additions, remodeling
repairing appliances
repairing furniture
car maintenance: change oil, tires, wash car
improvements to grounds

outdoor vegetable or flower gardening
care of houseplants
pet care: activities with pet, playing, walking
other indoor cleaning or repairs
other outdoor tasks
household paperwork: bills, mail, budget, checkbook
other household chores, picking things up at home
shopping for food, goods, durable household goods
activities related to buying/selling/renting house or apartment
activities related to financial services
activities related to government services
activities related to auto services
activities related to appliance repair
activities related to household repair service
travel related to obtaining goods and services
travel related to helping others
acquiring professional services
picking up food at takeout
obtaining other services

Leisure Activities

Television/radio
—listening to the radio
—watching television
—listening to records/tapes

Read
—reading books, magazines, newspapers, other

Hobbies/Games
—creative writing

—playing musical instrument
—singing
—acting, rehearsing
—non-social dancing
—preserving fruits and vegetables
—knitting
—sewing
—care of animals
—painting, potting, drawing
—playing cards, board games, social games
—puzzles

Organizations
—voluntary associations
—fraternal organizations
—political party, civic participation
—family organizations
—special interest organizations

Relaxing
—relaxing
—thinking, planning, reflecting

Sports
—team sports
—racquet sports
—golf, swimming, skating, skiing, bowling, pool, pinball
—frisbee, catch
—exercises, yoga
—boxing, wrestling, martial arts
—hunting, fishing
—boating, sailing, camping, beach

—snowmobiling

—flying, gliding

—pleasure drives, picnicking

—going for a walk, hiking, jogging, running, bicycling

—motorcycling, horseback riding

—photography

—work on car, repairing leisure equipment

—scrapbook, collection

—carpentry

—gymnastics, sports lessons

—travel for active leisure

Religion

—religious helping: meeting

—religious helping: other

—church group: other

—church group: meeting

—church services

—individual religious practice

Spectator Sports

—attending sports events

—other spectator events

Socializing

—going to parties

—going to a bar

—social dancing

—attending other social events

—travel for entertainment, socializing

Talking

—phone conversations

—other conversations

—conversations with household members

1987 NATIONAL SURVEY OF FAMILIES AND HOUSEHOLDS

Household Tasks

meal preparation

wash dishes

clean house

outdoor tasks

shopping

washing/ironing

paying bills

auto maintenance

driving

References

Auerbach, Judith D. 1990. "Employer-Supported Child Care as a Women–Responsive Policy," *Journal of Family Issues* 11(4):384–400.

Barrett, Nancy S. 1979. "Women in the Job Market: Occupations, Earnings and Career Opportunities." Pp. 31–61 in Ralph E. Smith (ed.) *The Subtle Revolution: Women at Work.* Washington DC: The Urban Institute.

Becker, Gary S. 1985. "Human Capital, Effort, and the Sexual Division of Labor," *Journal of Labor Economics* 3(1):S33–S58.

Becker, Gary S. 1981. *A Treatise on the Family.* Cambridge, MA: Harvard.

Becker, Gary S. 1975. *Human Capital* 2nd Edition. Chicago: University of Chicago Press.

Beckman, Linda J. and Betsy Bosak Houser. 1979. "The More You Have, the More You Do: The Relationship Between Wife's Employment, Sex–Role Attitudes, and Household Behavior," *Psychology of Women Quarterly* 4(2):160–174.

Berk, Richard A. and Sarah F. Berk. 1979. *Labor and Leisure at Home: Content and Organization of the Household Day.* Beverly Hills, CA: Sage.

Berk, Sarah F. 1985. *The Gender Factory: The Apportionment of Work in American Households.* New York: Plenum.

Berman, Eleanor. 1990. "Salute to a Real Family Man," *Working Mother* (June):50–53.

Bernard, Jesse. 1981. "The Good-Provider Role: Its Rise and Fall," *American Psychologist*, 36(1):1–12.

Blau, Francine D. and Marianne A. Ferber. 1986. *The Economics of Women, Men and Work*. Englewood Cliffs, NJ: Prentice Hall.

Blood, Robert O. and Donald M. Wolfe. 1960. *Husbands and Wives*. Glencoe, IL: Free Press.

Blumstein, Philip and Pepper Schwartz. 1991. "Money and Ideology: Their Impact on Power and the Division of Household Labor." Pp. 261–288 in Rae Lesser Blumberg (ed.) *Gender, Family, and Economy: The Triple Overlap*. Newbury Park, CA: Sage.

Blumstein, Philip and Pepper Schwartz. 1983. *American Couples: Money, Work, Sex*. New York: William Morrow.

Bollman, Stephan R., Virginia M. Moxley and Nancy C. Elliot. 1975. "Family and Community Activities of Rural Nonfarm Families with Children," *Journal of Leisure Research* 7(1):53–62.

Campbell, A. 1978. "Lifestyles, Free Time and Well-Being," *Leisure Work and the Family* 28–38. Stillwater, OK: Oklahoma State University. Pamphlet.

Christensen, Kathleen E. and Graham L. Staines. 1990. "Flextime: A Viable Solution to Work/Family Conflict?" *Journal of Family Issues* 11(4):455–476.

Clark, Robert A., F. Ivan Nye and Viktor Gecas. 1978. "Husbands' Work Involvement and Marital Role Performance," *Journal of Marriage and the Family* 40(1):9–21.

Coleman, Marion. 1991. "The Division of Household Labor: Suggestions for Future Empirical Consideration and Theoretical Development." Pp. 245–260 in Rae Lesser Blumberg (ed.) *Gender, Family, and Economy: The Triple Overlap*. Newbury Park, CA: Sage.

Coleman, Marion Tolbert and Jana M. Walters. 1989. "Beyond Gender Role Explanations: The Division of Household Labor in Gay and Lesbian Households." Paper presented at the Annual Meeting of the American Sociological Association, August 9–13.

Coverman, Shelley. 1985. "Explaining Husbands' Participation in Domestic Labor," *Sociological Quarterly* 26(1):81–97.

Coverman, Shelley and Joseph F. Sheley. 1986. "Change in Men's Housework and Child-Care Time, 1965-1975," *Journal of Marriage and the Family* 48(May):413-422.

Cunningham, Kenneth R. and Theodore B. Johannis. 1960. "Research on the Family and Leisure: A Review and Critique of Selected Studies," *The Family Life Coordinator* 9:25-32.

Davis, Margaret R. 1982. *Families in a Working World: The Impact of Organizations on Domestic Life.* New York: Praeger.

Deem, Rosemary. 1986. *All Work and No Play? The Sociology of Women and Leisure.* Milton Keynes, UK: Open University.

Deem, Rosemary. 1982. "Women, Leisure and Inequality," *Leisure Studies* 1(1):29-46.

Denmark, Florence L., Jeffrey S. Shaw and Samuel D. Ciali. 1985. "The Relationship Among Sex Roles, Living Arrangements and the Division of Household Responsibilities," *Sex Roles* 12(5-6):617-625.

Dowdall, Jean A. 1974. "Structural and Attitudinal Factors Associated with Female Labor-Force Participation," *Social Science Quarterly* 55:121-130.

England, Paula and George Farkas. 1986. *Households, Employment and Gender: A Social, Economic and Demographic View.* New York: Aldine.

Ericksen, Julia A., William L. Yancey and Eugene P. Ericksen. 1979. "The Division of Family Roles," *Journal of Marriage and the Family* 41:301-313.

Evans, Sara. 1980. *Personal Politics: The Roots of Women's Liberation in the Civil Rights Movement and The New Left.* New York: Knopf.

Farkas, George. 1976. "Education, Wage Rates, and the Division of Labor Between Husband and Wife," *Journal of Marriage and the Family* 38:473-483.

Fenstermaker, Sarah, Candace West and Don H. Zimmerman. 1991. "Gender Inequality: New Conceptual Terrain." Pp. 289-307 in Rae Lesser Blumberg (ed.) *Gender, Family and Economy: The Triple Overlap.* Newbury Park, CA: Sage.

Ferber, Marianne A. 1982. "Labor Market Participation of Young, Married Women: Causes and Effects," *Journal of Marriage and the Family* 44:457-468.

Ferree, Myra Marx. 1987. "Family and Job for Working-Class Women: Gender and Class Systems Seen from Below." Pp. 289–301 in Naomi Gerstel and Harriett Engel Gross (eds.) *Families and Work*. Philadelphia: Temple University.

Firestone, Juanita and Beth Anne Shelton. 1989. "The Impact of Wages on Labor Force Participation: Comparing Women and Men," *Sociology and Social Research* 74(2):127–136.

Firestone, Juanita and Beth Anne Shelton. 1988. "An Estimation of the Effect of Women's Work on Available Leisure Time," *Journal of Family Issues* 9(4):478–495.

Fox, Karen D. and Sharon Y. Nickols. 1983. "The Time Crunch: Wife's Employment and Family Work," *Journal of Family Issues* 4(1):61–82.

Galinsky, Ellen and Peter J. Stein. 1990. "The Impact of Human Resource Policies on Employees: Balancing Work/Family Life," *Journal of Family Issues*, 11(4):368–383.

Gauger, William. 1973. "Household Work: Can We Add It to the GNP?" *Journal of Home Economics* October:12–15.

Geerken, Michael and Walter R. Gove. 1983. *At Home and At Work: The Family's Allocation of Labor*. Beverly Hills: Sage.

Gentry, James W. and Mildred Doering. 1979. "Sex Role Orientation and Leisure," *Journal of Leisure Research* 11(2):102–111.

Gershuny, Jonathan and John P. Robinson. 1988. "Historical Changes in the Household Division of Labor," *Demography* 25(4):537–552.

Gerstel, Naomi and Harriet Engel Gross. 1989. "Women and the American Family: Continuity and Change." Pp. 89–120 in Jo Freeman (ed.) *Women: A Feminist Perspective* (4th Edition). Mountain View, CA: Mayfield.

Gerstel, Naomi and Harriet Engel Gross. 1987. "Commuter Marriage: A Microcosm of Career and Family Conflict." Pp. 422–433 in Naomi Gerstel and Harriet Engel Gross (eds.) *Families and Work*. Philadelphia: Temple University.

Glass, Becky L. 1988. "A Rational Choice Model of Wives' Employment Decisions," *Sociological Spectrum* 8:35–48.

Goldin, Claudia. 1989. "Life-Cycle Labor-Force Participation of Married Women: Historical Evidence and Implications," *Journal of Labor Economics* 7(1):20–47.

Greenberger, Ellen, Wendy A. Goldberg, Thomas J. Crawford and Jean Granger. 1988. "Beliefs About the Consequences of Maternal Employment for Children," *Psychology of Women Quarterly* 12:35–59.

Greenstein, Theodore. 1989. "Human Capital, Marital and Birth Timing, and the Postnatal Labor Force Participation of Married Women," *Journal of Family Issues* 10(3):359–382.

Greenstein, Theodore. 1986. "Social-Psychological Factors in Perinatal Labor-Force Participation," *Journal of Marriage and the Family* 48:565–571.

Grounau, Reuben. 1977. "Leisure, Home Production and Work—The Theory of the Allocation of Time Revisited," *Journal of Political Economy* 85(6):1099–1124.

Haas, Linda. 1990. "Gender Equality and Social Policy: Implications of a Study of Parental Leave in Sweden," *Journal of Family Issues* 11(4):401–423.

Hall, Trish. 1991. "Time on Your Hands? It May be Increasing," *New York Times* July 3, Section C1.

Hill, Martha S. 1985. "Investments of Time in Houses and Durables." Pp. 205–243 in F. Thomas Juster and Frank P. Stafford (eds.) *Time, Goods and Well-Being*. Ann Arbor, MI: Institute for Social Research.

Hochschild, Arlie. 1989. *The Second Shift: Working Parents and the Revolution at Home*. New York: Avon.

Huber, Joan and Glenna Spitze. 1983. *Sex Stratification: Children, Housework, and Jobs*. New York: Academic.

Hunt, Janet G. and Larry L. Hunt. 1987. "Male Resistance to Role Symmetry in Dual-Earner Households: Three Alternative Explanations." Pp. 192–203 in Naomi Gerstel and Harriet Engel Gross (eds.) *Families and Work*. Philadelphia: Temple University.

Juster, F. Thomas. 1985. "Investments of Time by Men and Women." Pp. 177–204 in F. Thomas Juster and Frank Stafford (eds.) *Time, Goods, and Well-Being*. Ann Arbor, MI: Institute for Social Research.

Juster, F. Thomas, Martha S. Hill, Frank P. Stafford and Jacqueline E. Parsons. 1983. *1975-1981 Time Use Longitudinal Panel Study*. Ann Arbor, MI: Inter-University Consortium for Political and Social Research.

Juster, F. Thomas and Frank P. Stafford. 1985. *Time, Goods, and Well-Being*. Ann Arbor, MI: Institute for Social Research.

Kilty, Keith M. and Virginia Richardson. 1985. "The Impact of Gender on Productive and Social Activities," *Journal of Sociology and Social Welfare* XII(1):162–185.

Kingston, Paul W. 1990. "Illusions and Ignorance About the Family-Responsive Workplace," *Journal of Family Issues* 11(4):438–454.

Koopman-Boyden, Peggy G. and Max Abbott. 1985. "Expectations for Household Task Allocation and Actual Task Allocation: A New Zealand Study," *Journal of Marriage and the Family* 47:211–219.

Lamb, Michael E. 1987. *The Father's Role: Cross-Cultural Perspectives*. Hillsdale, NJ: Lawrence Erlbaum.

Lamb, Michael E. 1987. "Introduction: The Emergent American Father." Pp. 3–25 in Michael E. Lamb (ed.) *The Father's Role: Cross-Cultural Perspectives*. Hillsdale, NJ: Lawrence Erlbaum.

Lamb, Michael E., Carl-Philip Hwang, Anders Broberg, Fred L. Bookstein, Gunilla Hult and Majt Frodj. 1988. "The Determinants of Paternal Involvement in Primiparous Swedish Families," *International Journal of Behavioral Development* 11(4):433–449.

LaRossa, Ralph. 1988. "Fatherhood and Social Change," *Family Relations* 37:451–457.

Leslie, Gerald. 1982. *The Family in Social Context* 5th Edition. New York: Oxford.

Lichter, Daniel T. and Janice A. Costanzo. 1987. "How Do Demographic Changes Affect Labor Force Participation for Women?" *Monthly Labor Review* 110(11):23–25.

Locksley, Anne. 1980. "On the Effects of Wives' Employment on Marital Adjustment and Companionship," *Journal of Marriage and the Family* 42:337–346.

Lopata, Helen Z., Debra Barnewolt and Kathleen Norr. 1980. "Spouses' Contributions to Each Other's Roles." Pp. 111–142 in Fran Pepitone-Rockwell (ed.) *Dual Career Couples*. Beverly Hills, CA: Sage.

Lorence, Jon. 1987. "Subjective Labor Force Commitment of U.S. Men and Women, 1973–1985," *Social Science Quarterly* 68(4):745–760.

Marini, Margaret Mooney and Beth Anne Shelton. 1991. "Measuring Household Work: Recent Experience in the United States," unpublished manuscript.

McAllister, Ian. 1990. "Gender and the Division of Labor: Employment and Earnings Variations in Australia," *Work and Occupations* 17(1):79–99.

McLaughlin, Steven D. 1982. "Differential Patterns of Female Labor-Force Participation Surrounding First Birth," *Journal of Marriage and the Family* 44:407–420.

Meissner, Martin, Elizabeth W. Humphries, Scott M. Meis and William J. Scheu. 1975. "No Exit for Wives: Sexual Division of Labor and the Cumulation of Household Demands," *Canadian Review of Sociology and Anthropology* 12:424–439.

Miller, Joanne and Howard H. Garrison. 1982. "Sex Roles: The Division of Labor at Home and in the Workplace," *Annual Review of Sociology* 8:237–262.

Model, Suzanne. 1981. "Housework by Husbands: Determinants and Implications," *Journal of Family Issues* 2(2):225–237.

Moore, H. and Janice Niepert Hedges. 1971. "Trends in Labor and Leisure," *Monthly Labor Review* 94:3–11.

"New Kind of Life with Father." 1981, November 30. Pp. 93–94, *Newsweek*.

Newcomb, Michael D. 1983. "Relationship Qualities of Those Who Live Together," *Alternative Lifestyles* 6(2):78–102.

Nock, Steven L. and Paul William Kingston. 1989. "The Division of Leisure and Work," *Social Science Quarterly* 70(1):24–39.

Nock, Steven L. and Paul William Kingston. 1988. "Time with Children: The Impact of Couples' Work-Time Commitments," *Social Forces* 67(1):59–85.

Nye, F. Ivan. 1963. "The Adjustment of Adolescent Children." Pp. 133–141 in F. Ivan Nye and Lois W. Hoffman (eds.) *The Employed Mother in America*. Chicago: Rand McNally.

Oakley, Ann. 1974. *Women's Work: The Housewife, Past and Present*. New York: Vintage.

O'Connell, Martin. 1990. "Maternity Leave Arrangements: 1961–1985." Pp. 11–27 in *Work and Family Patterns of American*

Women. Washington DC: U.S. Department of Commerce, Current Population Reports, Special Studies Series P-23, No. 165.

Oppenheimer, Valerie Kincade. 1982. *Work and the Family: A Study in Social Demography.* New York: Academic Press.

Parker, Stanley. 1976. *The Sociology of Leisure.* New York: International.

Parsons, Talcott and Robert F. Bales. 1955. *Family, Socialization, and Interaction Process.* Glencoe, IL: Free Press.

Perrucci, Carolyn, Harry R. Potter and Deborah C. Rhoads. 1978. "Determinants of Male Family-Role Performance," *Psychology of Women Quarterly* 3(1):53–66.

Pleck, Joseph. 1990. "Family Supportive Employer Policies: Are They Relevant to Men?" Paper presented at the American Psychological Association, Boston, MA, August 12.

Pleck, Joseph. 1989. "Family-Supportive Employer Policies and Men's Participation." Paper presented at National Research Council Panel on Employer Policies and Working Families, Committee on Women's Employment and Related Social Issues, March 20–21.

Pleck, Joseph. 1985. *Working Wives, Working Husbands.* Beverly Hills, CA: Sage.

Pleck, Joseph. 1977. "The Work Family Role System," *Social Problems* 24(4):417–427.

Powell, Brian and Lala Carr Steelman. 1982. "Testing an Undertested Comparison: Maternal Effects on Sons' and Daughters' Attitudes Toward Women in the Labor Force," *Journal of Marriage and the Family* 44:349–355.

Record, Ann Elise and Marjorie E. Starrels. 1990. "Gender and Generational Divisions of Housework: Patterns and Explanations." Paper presented at the annual meeting of the American Sociological Association, August 23–27.

Reskin, Barbara and Patricia A. Roos. 1987. "Status Hierarchies and Sex Segregation." Pp. 3–21 in Christine Bose and Glenna Spitze (eds.) *Ingredients of Women's Employment Policy.* Albany, NY: State University of New York.

Rexroat, Cynthia. 1990. "Race and Marital Status Differences in the Labor Force Behavior of Female Family Heads: The Effect of

Household Structure," *Journal of Marriage and the Family* 52:591–601.

Robinson, John P. 1977. *How Americans Use Time: A Social-Psychological Analysis of Everyday Behavior.* New York: Praeger.

Robinson, John P. 1988. "Who's Doing the Housework?" *American Demographics* 10:24–63.

Ross, Catherine E. 1987. "The Division of Labor at Home," *Social Forces* 65(3):816–833.

Rubin, Lillian B. 1976. *Worlds of Pain: Life in the Working-Class Family.* New York: Basic Books.

Sanik, Margaret Mietus. 1981. "Division of Household Work: A Decade Comparison—1967–1977," *Home Economics Research Journal* 10:175–180.

Schooler, Carmi, Joanne Miller, Karen A. Miller and Carol N. Richland. 1984. "Work for the Household: Its Nature and Consequences for Husbands and Wives," *American Journal of Sociology* 90(1):97–124.

Schwartz, Felice N. 1989. "Management Women and the New Facts of Life," *Harvard Business Review* 67:65–76.

Shamir, Boas. 1986. "Unemployment and Household Division of Labor," *Journal of Marriage and the Family* 48(February):195–206.

Shank, John W. 1986. "An Exploration of Leisure in the Lives of Dual Career Women," *Journal of Leisure Research* 18(4):300–319.

Shaw, Susan. 1986. "Leisure, Recreation or Free Time? Measuring Time Usage," *Journal of Leisure Research* 18(3):177–189.

Shaw, Susan. 1985. "Gender and Leisure: Inequality in the Distribution of Leisure Time," *Journal of Leisure Research* 17(4):266–282.

Shelton, Beth Anne. 1990. "The Distribution of Household Tasks: Does Wife's Employment Status Make a Difference?" *Journal of Family Issues* 11(2):115–135.

Shelton, Beth Anne and Shelley Coverman. 1988. "Estimating Change in Husbands' Domestic Labor Time." Paper presented at the Annual Meeting of the American Sociological Association, August 24–28.

Shelton, Beth Anne and Juanita Firestone. 1988. "An Examination of Household Labor Time as a Factor in Composition and Treatment Effects on the Male-Female Wage Gap," *Sociological Focus* 21(3):265–278.

Smith, James P. and Michael P. Ward. 1984. *Women's Wages and Work in the Twentieth Century* Rand Report R-3119-NICHD. Santa Monica, CA: The Rand Corporation.

Smith, Ralph. 1979. *The Subtle Revolution: Women at Work.* Washington DC: The Urban Institute.

Sorensen, Annemette and Sara McLanahan. 1987. "Married Women's Economic Dependency: 1940-1980," *American Journal of Sociology* 93(3):659–687.

Spitze, Glenna. 1988. "The Data on Women's Labor Force Participation." Pp. 42–60 in Ann Helton Stromberg and Shirley Harkess (eds.) *Working Women: Theories and Facts in Perspective,* 2nd Edition. Mountain View, CA: Mayfield.

Spitze, Glenna. 1986. "The Division of Task Responsibility in U. S. Households: Longitudinal Adjustments to Change," *Social Forces* 64(3):689–701.

Sporkin, Elizabeth and Maria Speidel. 1991. "Correspondent Meredith Viera Asks for a '60 Minutes' Pregnancy Break—And CBS Lets Her Time Run Out," *People* March 18:71–72.

Sprague, Alison. 1988. "Post-war Fertility and Female Labour Force Rates," *The Economic Journal* 98:682–700.

Stafford, Rebecca, Elaine Backman and Pamela Dibona. 1977. "The Division of Labor Among Cohabiting and Married Couples," *Journal of Marriage and the Family* 39:43–57.

Suitor, J. Jill. 1991. "Marital Quality and Satisfaction with the Division of Household Labor Across the Family Life Cycle," *Journal of Marriage and the Family* 53(1):221–230.

Sweet, James, Lawrence Bumpass and Vaughn Call. 1988. "The Design and Content of the *National Survey of Families and Households*" Working Paper NSFH-1. Madison, WI: Center for Demography and Economy, University of Wisconsin.

Szinovacz, Maximiliane. 1977. "Role Allocation, Family Structure and Female Employment," *Journal of Marriage and the Family* 39(February):781–791.

Tinsley, Howard E.A. and Thomas L. Johnson. 1984. "A Preliminary Taxonomy of Leisure Activities," *Journal of Leisure Research* 16(3):234–244.

Tolman, Audrey E., Kristina A. Diekman and Kathleen McCartney. 1989. "Social Connectedness and Mothering: Effects of Maternal Employment and Maternal Absence," *Journal of Personality and Social Psychology* 56(6):942-949.

Trost, Cathy. 1988. "Men, Too, Wrestle with Career Family Stress," *Wall Street Journal* November 1:33.

United Media Enterprises Report on Leisure in America. 1982. *Where Does the Time Go?* New York: United Media Enterprises.

Vanek, Joann. 1984. "Housewives as Workers." Pp. 89-103 in Patricia Voydanoff (ed.) *Work and Family: Changing Roles for Men and Women*. Palo Alto, CA: Mayfield.

Vanek, Joann. 1974. "Time Spent in Housework," *Scientific American* 231(5):116-120.

Waite, Linda J. 1981. "U.S. Women at Work," *Population Bulletin* 36:3-43.

Waite, Linda J. 1980. "Working Wives and the Family Life Cycle," *American Journal of Sociology* 86:272-294.

Waite, Linda J. and Ross M. Stolzenberg. 1976. "Intended Childbearing and Labor-Force Participation of Young Women: Insights from Nonrecursive Models," *American Sociological Review* 41:235-252.

Wall Street Journal. 1988. "Labor Letter," *Wall Street Journal* July 19:1.

Wethington, Elaine and Ronald C. Kessler. 1989. "Employment, Parental Responsibility and Psychological Distress: A Longitudinal Study of Married Women," *Journal of Family Issues* 10(4):527-546.

Yllo, Kersti Alice. 1978. "Nonmarital Cohabitation: Beyond the College Campus," *Alternative Lifestyles* 1(1):37-54.

Young, Michael Dunlop and Peter Willmott. 1973. *The Symmetrical Family*. New York: Pantheon.

Index

About the Author

BETH ANNE SHELTON is Associate Professor of Sociology at the State University of New York at Buffalo. An authority on the sociology of gender, she has published extensively, including articles in the *Journal of Marriage and the Family*, *Gender & Society*, and the *Journal of Family Issues*.